Gavin Campbell

Tuatha Dé Da
Guardians of the Emerald Isle

Unearthing Ireland's Mythologies, Folklore & Magic

Copyright © 2023 Gavin Campbell Books, All rights reserved.

No part of this publication, authored by Gavin Campbell Books, may be reproduced, distributed, or transmitted in any form or by any means, including photocopying, recording, or other electronic or mechanical methods, without the prior written permission of the publisher, except in the case of brief quotations embodied in reviews and certain other non-commercial uses permitted by copyright law.

ISBN: 9798860009714

This extended copyright disclaimer explicitly highlights that "Gavin Campbell Books" is the author of the work and emphasizes their ownership and exclusive rights to the publication. The added information reinforces the importance of obtaining written permission from the publisher before any reproduction, distribution, or transmission of the content, while also acknowledging the possibility of brief quotations for specific purposes as permitted by copyright law.

About the Author

I am Gavin Campbell, hailing from the picturesque County of Louth in the heart of Ireland. My journey as a writer began with the creation of children's books, where I delighted in crafting tales that would ignite young imaginations. However, as the pages turned, my own storytelling horizons expanded, beckoning me into the enchanting world of fiction.

The genesis of my latest venture, the book you now hold, was a fascination that consumed my every thought—the Tuatha Dé Danann. These mythic beings, steeped in the history, myth, and folklore of Ireland, captivated my curiosity like no other subject before. It was a journey born of research, one that began with the intent of incorporating them into a work of fiction. Little did I know that this pursuit would lead me on an odyssey of exploration, immersion, and revelation.

The allure of the Tuatha Dé Danann is not confined to their mystic legacy; it transcends the realms of time and place. As I delved deeper into their story, I found myself ensnared by the rich tapestry of Irish history and myth that wove their tale. It was an odyssey that drew me into the depths of ancient Ireland, where gods, magic, and heroes once walked the land.

As you turn the pages of this book, I invite you to join me on this mythic voyage, to immerse yourself in the history, the magic, and the enduring allure of the Tuatha Dé Danann. In their story, we find a tapestry of human experience—of triumph and adversity, of gods and mortals, of a land where myth and reality intertwine. It is my hope that you will come to know these mythic beings not as mere legends of a bygone era, but as timeless companions on a journey through the captivating world of Irish mythology.

Thank you for embarking on this adventure with me. May the stories within these pages resonate in your heart as they have in mine, and may the spirit of the Tuatha Dé Danann continue to enchant and inspire us all.

Table of Contents

Introduction..05

Chapter 1: Mythological Origins...10

Chapter 2: The Divine Pantheon..23

Chapter 3: The Four Treasures of the Tuatha Dé Danann............61

Chapter 4: Kingship and Leadership...65

Chapter 5: Devine Battles for Ireland and the Exodus to the Otherworld........70

Chapter 6: The Tuatha Dé Danann & Their Enduring Connection to Irish Landmarks..84

Chapter 7: Otherworldly Realms...91

Chapter 8: Symbolism and Themes..95

Chapter 9: Magic, Craftsmanship, and Skills................................97

Chapter 10: Relationships and Interactions................................101

Chapter 11: Influence on Irish Culture..103

Chapter 12: Imbolc and Other Festivals.....................................108

Chapter 13: Modern Interpretations..113

Chapter 14: Unanswered Questions and Speculations..............119

Conclusion..123

Introduction

The Allure of Irish Mythology

Irish mythology weaves a captivating tapestry of enchanting stories, heroic feats, and mystical beings that have enthralled generations. Nestled within this intricate web of tales lies the enigmatic allure of the Tuatha Dé Danann, a group of divine beings whose stories have transcended time and geography to become an integral part of global mythology. As we embark on a journey to unravel the secrets and wonders of the Tuatha Dé Danann, we are drawn into the profound magic of Irish mythology, a realm where history and imagination converge.

1. Myth and Mystery: At the heart of Irish mythology is the interplay between myth and mystery. These ancient stories are not merely fragments of the past, but rather windows into a world of symbolism, metaphor, and deeper meanings. The allure of Irish mythology lies in its ability to tantalize our curiosity, inviting us to decipher hidden truths and uncover the layers of wisdom concealed beneath the surface of each tale. The Tuatha Dé Danann embody this mystique, with their divine lineage, magical powers, and connections to the Otherworld sparking our imagination and beckoning us to explore the unknown.

2. Cultural Identity and Legacy: Irish mythology is not just a collection of stories; it's a mirror reflecting the cultural identity and historical consciousness of the Irish people. The Tuatha Dé Danann are more than legendary figures; they are an intrinsic part of Ireland's collective memory and heritage. Through the centuries, these myths have been woven into the fabric of Irish society, influencing art, literature, and even political discourse. The allure of the Tuatha Dé Danann and their stories stems from their role as guardians of cultural identity, reminding us of the ancient roots that shape modern Ireland.

3. The Eternal and the Ethereal: One of the captivating aspects of Irish mythology is its ability to blur the lines between the eternal and the ethereal. The Tuatha Dé Danann are not confined to a distant past; they live on in the poetic verses, folklore, and traditions of today. The allure lies in their timeless quality, how they continue to enchant and resonate across generations. Their residence in the Otherworld, a realm beyond

mortal understanding, bridges the gap between the earthly and the divine, offering us a glimpse of a reality that transcends the mundane.

4. Universal Themes and Human Experience: While rooted in Irish culture, the wonder of Irish mythology extends beyond national borders. The stories of the Tuatha Dé Danann touch on universal themes that resonate with the human experience: heroism, love, sacrifice, and the quest for wisdom. These themes are vehicles through which we explore our own emotions, desires, and aspirations. The tales of the Tuatha Dé Danann provide a lens through which we examine the complexity of human nature, fostering connections across time and space.

5. The Unseen and the Unspoken: In the realm of Irish mythology, what remains unsaid often speaks the loudest. The enchantment of the Tuatha Dé Danann lies in the gaps between the lines, the silences that leave room for interpretation. It's in these spaces that our own creativity finds room to flourish, as we imagine the untold stories, motivations, and emotions that shape the characters and events. The allure is in the unspoken truths that echo through the ages, inviting us to fill in the blanks with our own insights and perspectives.

In embarking on this journey to explore the Tuatha Dé Danann, we venture into a realm of wonder and fascination. Irish mythology is in the way it transcends time, space, and culture, drawing us into a world where the tangible and the intangible coalesce, where history mingles with imagination, and where the stories of the Tuatha Dé Danann continue to weave their enchanting spell.

6. Imagination and Connection: Irish mythology resides in its capacity to ignite our imagination and kindle a sense of connection with the past. As we delve into the stories of the Tuatha Dé Danann, we find ourselves transported to a time when the boundary between the ordinary and the extraordinary was fluid. These tales transport us to a world where gods walked among mortals, where magic was a tangible force, and where destinies were intertwined with the threads of fate. The allure lies in our ability to step into this world through the power of storytelling, forging a bond with those who came before us and those who will follow.

7. Layers of Interpretation: Irish mythology is like a prism that refracts light into a spectrum of interpretations. The stories of the Tuatha Dé Danann

are not static narratives, but dynamic tapestries that reveal new facets with each examination. The wonder and captivation lies in the layers of meaning waiting to be discovered—psychological, spiritual, allegorical. These stories beckon us to peel back the layers, to explore the depths of symbolism, and to find resonance with our own personal journeys.

8. Lessons from the Divine: Beyond their ethereal attributes, the Tuatha Dé Danann offer valuable lessons that resonate with contemporary life. Their tales embody timeless principles of leadership, sacrifice, courage, and the pursuit of knowledge. The allure of these stories lies in their capacity to offer guidance and insight, prompting us to reflect on how the virtues and challenges faced by these divine beings mirror our own experiences and dilemmas.

9. Living Legacy: The allure of Irish mythology and the stories of the Tuatha Dé Danann is not confined to dusty tomes of the past. They continue to breathe life into contemporary culture, shaping the narratives of today. Whether through literature, music, visual art, or even digital media, the legacy of the Tuatha Dé Danann persists, finding new expressions in every generation. The dynamic interplay between ancient myth and modern creativity, bridging the temporal gap and infusing these tales with enduring relevance.

In exploring the wonder of Irish mythology, we begin a journey that traverses both time and imagination. The Tuatha Dé Danann, with their shimmering silver arms, their otherworldly realms, and their timeless wisdom, beckon us to explore the depths of their stories and the richness of their significance. As we navigate the pages of this book, we find ourselves in the embrace of an enchanting legacy that spans centuries—a legacy that continues to cast its spell upon all who dare to venture into the realm of the Tuatha Dé Danann.

Purpose and Structure of the Book

The purpose of this book is to unravel the captivating world of the Tuatha Dé Danann, the divine beings who have captured the imagination of generations with their enchanting tales and timeless significance. As we embark on this journey, the book aims to achieve several key objectives:

Revelation of Hidden Myths and Insights: The Tuatha Dé Danann, often shrouded in the mists of time and myth, have long been the subjects of fascination and curiosity. Through meticulous research and analysis of ancient texts, folklore, and cultural references, this book aims to unearth hidden myths, forgotten stories, and previously undiscovered insights into the lives and roles of these remarkable beings.

Cultural and Historical Context: Understanding the Tuatha Dé Danann goes beyond mere storytelling; it is an exploration of Irish culture, history, and spirituality. By delving into their myths and symbols, we can gain a deeper understanding of the beliefs, values, and worldview of the people who conceived them. This book seeks to provide readers with a contextual framework that enriches their comprehension of the Tuatha Dé Danann's impact on Irish identity and heritage.

Interpretation and Modern Relevance: The stories of the Tuatha Dé Danann have transcended time, influencing literature, art, and popular culture through the ages. This book endeavors to offer insightful interpretations of these tales, shedding light on their meanings, symbolism, and relevance in the modern world. By examining how these myths have evolved and resonated with different generations, we can gain a greater appreciation for their enduring significance.

Empowerment Through Knowledge: Beyond the realm of myth and folklore, the Tuatha Dé Danann have served as archetypes, embodying qualities such as courage, wisdom, and resilience. This book seeks to empower readers by illuminating the transformative lessons that can be drawn from their stories. By exploring the challenges they faced and the choices they made, we can find inspiration to navigate our own journeys with strength and purpose.

Significance and Cultural Impact of the Tuatha Dé Danann

The Tuatha Dé Danann as depicted in John Duncan's *Riders of the Sidhe* (1911)

The Tuatha Dé Danann occupy a special place in the rich tapestry of Irish mythology, a cultural heritage that has captivated the imagination of generations. Their significance extends beyond mere characters in tales; they embody the essence of Ireland's mythical past, representing the interplay between mortal and divine, nature and magic, and the ongoing narrative of cultural identity.

The Tuatha Dé Danann serve as a bridge connecting the mortal realm to the divine. As deities with human-like qualities, they offer a glimpse into the human desire to understand the mysteries of the cosmos, the forces that shape existence, and the existence of beings beyond human comprehension. Their stories explore themes of heroism, sacrifice, and the intricate relationships between gods and humans, painting a vivid portrait of the intersection of the divine and the mundane.

In the preliterate times of ancient Ireland, oral storytelling was the primary medium for passing down traditions, beliefs, and history. The stories of the Tuatha Dé Danann were the threads that wove together the fabric of community and identity. Bards and storytellers held the responsibility of preserving and transmitting these narratives, ensuring that the tales remained alive in the hearts and minds of each generation.

The mythological landscape of Ireland is profoundly intertwined with the stories of the Tuatha Dé Danann. Mythical sites, often known as "fairy mounds" or "sidhe," are believed to be entrances to the Otherworld, where the Tuatha Dé Danann reside. These locations are not merely physical landmarks; they are gateways to a realm of wonder, mystery, and magic. The presence of these mythical sites has influenced the geographical and cultural tapestry of Ireland, leaving an indelible mark on the collective imagination. The tales of the Tuatha Dé Danann have inspired countless works of literature, poetry, and art throughout the ages. From medieval manuscripts and poetic compositions to contemporary novels and paintings, their stories have served as a wellspring of creative inspiration. Through these expressions, artists and writers have explored themes of identity, spirituality, and the timeless struggle between order and chaos.

Continuity and Evolution: From Ancient Myth to Modern Identity
The enduring allure of the Tuatha Dé Danann lies not only in their historical roots but also in their adaptability to changing times. As Ireland transitioned through different eras, from pre-Christian paganism to Christianity and beyond, the Tuatha Dé Danann's tales evolved while retaining their essential core. This evolution speaks to the resilience of cultural heritage, the ability to incorporate new perspectives, and the capacity to find relevance in the ever-shifting currents of history.

In essence, the Tuatha Dé Danann are more than mythological figures; they are symbolic embodiments of Ireland's collective consciousness. They represent the yearning for connection with the divine, the deep reverence for nature, and the unbreakable bond between a people and their stories. As we journey through their myths and legends, we embark on a quest to understand not only the past, but also the enduring spirit that continues to shape the cultural identity of Ireland and its people. Beyond their divine qualities, the stories of the Tuatha Dé Danann also contain valuable ethical lessons and reflections on human behavior. Their struggles, triumphs, and interactions often serve as allegories for real-world challenges, offering insights into courage, wisdom, justice, and the consequences of one's actions. Through the lens of these mythical beings, listeners and readers are prompted to consider the choices they make and the impact those choices have on their lives and communities.

The legacy of the Tuatha Dé Danann spans centuries, binding generations together through a shared connection to their tales. This continuity of storytelling fosters a sense of belonging and continuity, as the stories are passed down from parents to children, from teachers to students. This intergenerational exchange maintains a living link to the past, preserving not only the stories themselves but also the values, wisdom, and sense of wonder they encapsulate.

A Source of Cultural Resilience

Throughout history, Ireland has faced periods of upheaval, colonization, and social change. In times of uncertainty, the stories of the Tuatha Dé Danann have served as a wellspring of cultural resilience. Their tales provide solace, inspiration, and a reminder of the enduring spirit that can weather storms and adapt to changing circumstances. The Tuatha Dé Danann, through their struggles and triumphs, mirror the resilience of the Irish people themselves.

The tales of the Tuatha Dé Danann also facilitate a dialogue between the mythic realm and the realities of the human experience. The Otherworldly interactions, the mysteries of magic, and the interconnectedness of the mortal and divine challenge us to contemplate the boundaries of the known and the unknown. In these stories, the extraordinary and the ordinary coexist, allowing us to explore the mysteries of existence through a lens of imagination and wonder.

As we delve deeper into the stories of the Tuatha Dé Danann, we embark on a journey that transcends time and space. With each tale, we uncover layers of meaning, symbol, and metaphor that reflect not only the ancient past but also the universal themes that resonate with human experience. By exploring their myths, we not only learn about the gods and goddesses themselves but also embark on a quest to understand ourselves, our world, and the enduring quest for meaning that unites all of humanity.

In the pages ahead, we will unravel the intricacies of the Tuatha Dé Danann's history, the enchantment of their stories, and the profound impact they have had on Irish culture and identity. Through meticulous research, thoughtful analysis, and a journey into the heart of mythology, I aim to illuminate the significance of the Tuatha Dé Danann in a way that resonates with readers and invites them to partake in the timeless tradition of storytelling that continues to shape the world around us.

Chapter 1
Mythological Origins

The Celtic Origins of the Tuatha Dé Danann

The roots of the Tuatha Dé Danann trace back to the heart of Celtic mythology, a rich tapestry woven with ancient beliefs, traditions, and stories. These origins are shrouded in mystery, interwoven with the landscape of prehistoric Ireland and the imaginations of its people.

In Celtic cosmology, the world was not only a physical realm but also a spiritual domain intertwined with the supernatural. The Celts believed that the land, rivers, and even the sky held spirits and deities, forming an interconnected web that influenced daily life. Within this intricate tapestry, the Tuatha Dé Danann emerged as a divine race, embodying the divine essence of the land and its inhabitants.

The mythology tells of the Tuatha Dé Danann arriving in Ireland from distant lands, often associated with the Celtic Otherworld. This arrival was not a mere migration, but a cosmic event that blurred the lines between the mortal realm and the supernatural. The Tuatha Dé Danann were perceived as beings of immense power, descending from the heavens or emerging from the depths of the earth, signifying a sacred connection between worlds.

The Tuatha Dé Danann were considered descendants of the goddess Danu, the mother figure from whom their name is derived. This divine lineage endowed them with a unique status, marking them as divine beings with a direct link to the primordial forces that shaped the universe. Their ancestry connected them to cosmic cycles, emphasizing their role as intermediaries between the physical and spiritual realms.

The mythological narratives that surround the Tuatha Dé Danann offer glimpses into their origins and interactions with other mythological beings. These narratives, often intertwined with the natural landscape of Ireland, shaped the way the Celts perceived their world. Stories of battles, alliances, and interactions with beings like the Fomorians added depth to the Tuatha Dé Danann's mythological identity.

The Symbolism of Arrival and Integration

The arrival of the Tuatha Dé Danann carried profound symbolism, reflecting themes of migration, cultural integration, and the dynamic interaction between different peoples and belief systems. Their stories served as a reflection of the societal changes and interactions that ancient Celtic communities experienced, making them more than mere mythological figures — they became vessels for understanding the complexities of the world.

To fully grasp the Celtic origins of the Tuatha Dé Danann, it's crucial to consider the historical and cultural context in which these myths evolved. The Celts were a diverse group of peoples with a shared cultural framework, yet each tribe and region contributed to the evolution of these myths. Their cosmology, oral traditions, and reverence for nature all played a role in shaping the narrative tapestry that birthed the Tuatha Dé Danann.

In exploring the Celtic origins of the Tuatha Dé Danann, we unravel threads that connect the divine with the mortal, the ancient with the present, and the physical with the spiritual. These origins set the stage for the rich tapestry of myth and meaning that the Tuatha Dé Danann would become in the landscape of Irish mythology.

Sacred Landscapes and Mythic Realms

The Celtic origins of the Tuatha Dé Danann are intricately woven into the landscape of Ireland itself. The hills, rivers, and ancient structures of the land were not only physical features but also gateways to the supernatural. Places like the ancient mounds and hills of Ireland were believed to be thresholds between the mortal realm and the Otherworld, where the Tuatha Dé Danann resided.

As the Tuatha Dé Danann settled into Ireland, their interactions with mortals were considered pivotal moments in Celtic mythology. Their benevolent gifts of knowledge, magic, and craftsmanship often served as markers of their divine origins. Mortals who crossed paths with these beings were often granted insights into the sacred and profound, highlighting the intricate ways in which the divine and human spheres intertwined.

The Celtic origins of the Tuatha Dé Danann were preserved through a combination of oral tradition and, eventually, written records. The oral tradition was a conduit through which myths were passed down from generation to generation, evolving with each retelling while retaining core themes and messages. With the advent of written records, these stories were captured in manuscripts, reflecting the intricate weaving of cultural memory and literary artistry.

The Tuatha Dé Danann were more than just mythological figures; they embodied the Celtic worldview, acting as bridges between the tangible and intangible, the natural and supernatural. Their arrival from the Otherworld to the mortal realm mirrored the ebb and flow of the seasons, symbolizing the cyclical nature of life, death, and rebirth. This bridge-building quality highlighted the interconnectedness of all existence.

Legacy and Continuing Reverence

The Celtic origins of the Tuatha Dé Danann continue to shape the spiritual and cultural landscape of Ireland and beyond. These ancient tales hold a mirror to the human experience, reflecting themes of heroism, sacrifice, and the quest for understanding the mysteries of life. The legacy of the Tuatha Dé Danann echoes in modern-day festivals, artwork, and literature, emphasizing their enduring relevance.

The Celtic origins of the Tuatha Dé Danann remain a subject of fascination, scholarly inquiry, and creative exploration. As archaeological discoveries, linguistic analyses, and cultural studies deepen our understanding of the Ancient Celts, they provide new lenses through which to interpret the origins and significance of these divine beings. The quest to uncover the truths of the past is an ongoing journey, one that enriches our appreciation of the Tuatha Dé Danann's place within the tapestry of Celtic mythology.

In delving into the Celtic origins of the Tuatha Dé Danann, we peel back the layers of time and immerse ourselves in the heart of an ancient belief system. These origins illuminate the interconnectedness of mythology, culture, and the natural world, offering a glimpse into the spiritual landscape of the Celtic peoples and the enduring mysteries that continue to captivate our imaginations.

Their Arrival in Ireland: Myth and Mystery

The story of the Tuatha Dé Danann's arrival in Ireland is shrouded in myth and mystery, intertwining history and folklore to create a narrative that reflects the deep connection between the divine and the earthly. This part of their mythological origins explores the enigmatic circumstances of their arrival and the significance of this event in Celtic mythology.

The Tuatha Dé Danann were said to hail from the Otherworld, often referred to as the land of the Sidhe. The origins of the Sidhe are deeply rooted in the ancient beliefs and traditions of the Celts, the early inhabitants of Ireland. The word "Sidhe" is believed to be derived from the Old Irish term "síd," which originally referred to burial mounds or barrows. These ancient burial sites were believed to be portals or gateways to the Otherworld, the realm inhabited by the Sidhe. Over time, the concept of the Sidhe evolved, and they came to be seen as supernatural beings with their own distinct society and characteristics.

The Sidhe are depicted as a race of supernatural beings who exist in a parallel world, often referred to as the Otherworld or Tir na nÓg. They are typically described as tall and fair, with an otherworldly beauty that sets them apart from mortal humans. In Irish folklore, it is believed that the Sidhe live in grand underground palaces or forts known as "sídhe mounds" or "fairy forts," which are hidden from human sight. These mounds are said to be entrances to the Otherworld, and they are scattered throughout the Irish landscape.

The Sidhe are known for their magical abilities, particularly in the realms of music, healing, and shape-shifting. They are skilled musicians, and their enchanting music is said to have the power to mesmerize and transport humans to the Otherworld. Additionally, the Sidhe are often associated with the natural world, with some stories depicting them as protectors of the land and its creatures. They are believed to have the ability to heal and bless, but they can also be capricious and vengeful if provoked or offended.

One of the most enduring characteristics of the Sidhe is their propensity for meddling in the affairs of mortals. They are known to interact with humans, often appearing as beautiful, alluring beings who can be both helpful and mischievous. In Irish folklore, it is said that encountering the Sidhe can lead to both great fortune and great misfortune, and many cautionary tales warn against offending or crossing these supernatural beings.

The Sidhe have left an indelible mark on Irish culture and folklore, and their presence is still felt today. Countless stories, legends, and folktales feature the Sidhe as central characters or themes. These tales often explore the interaction between the mortal world and the Otherworld, highlighting the blurred boundaries between the two realms.

One well-known Sidhe-related legend is the story of the "Changeling." In this narrative, it is believed that the Sidhe would steal human infants and replace them with their own changeling children. These changelings were often sickly or mischievous, and they served as a cautionary tale to parents. This legend reflects the age-old belief in the Sidhe's ability to influence the lives of mortals.

The Sidhe also feature prominently in Irish poetry and literature. Renowned Irish poets such as W.B. Yeats drew inspiration from the Sidhe in their works, capturing the mystical and ethereal qualities of these supernatural beings. Yeats' collection of poems titled "The Celtic Twilight" explores the theme of the Sidhe and their connection to Irish folklore and national identity.

According to some versions of the mythology, the Tuatha Dé Danann arrived in Ireland in a series of invasions. They were believed to have encountered and defeated the Fir Bolg, an earlier group of inhabitants, establishing their presence in the land. This marked the beginning of their influential role in Irish mythology and history.

Among the Tuatha Dé Danann, Nuada Airgetlám emerged as a leader and king. His leadership was marked by his wisdom, just governance, and the air of divine authority. Nuada's reign during this period was relatively peaceful and prosperous, laying the foundation for the Tuatha Dé Danann's enduring impact on Irish culture.

The arrival of the Tuatha Dé Danann was not simply a geographical migration; it represented a merging of ancient deities and mythological beings with the land of Ireland. These divine figures brought with them their own stories, powers, and traditions, which would go on to influence the tapestry of Irish mythology.

The mythological origins of the Tuatha Dé Danann's arrival are closely intertwined with Ireland's historical context. The stories of divine beings arriving in the land speak to the Celtic people's deep connection to their homeland and the sense of divine inheritance. These myths also provided a framework for understanding the shifting power dynamics and interactions between different groups in ancient times.

The concept of the Otherworld and the Tuatha Dé Danann's arrival highlights the permeable boundary between the mortal world and the mystical realm. The veil between these worlds is thin, and the Tuatha Dé Danann's presence in Ireland reinforced the belief in the interplay between the seen and the unseen, the mortal and the divine.

The myth of the Tuatha Dé Danann's arrival in Ireland carries profound symbolic meaning. Their journey is not just a narrative of migration but also a reflection of the perpetual cycle of life, death, and rebirth. It embodies themes of renewal, transformation, and the enduring connection between the divine and the mortal.

The myth and mystery surrounding the Tuatha Dé Danann's arrival in Ireland capture the essence of Celtic mythology—a blend of history and folklore that reflects the complex relationship between the divine and the human. This pivotal event laid the foundation for the Tuatha Dé Danann's influence on Irish culture, and their story continues to inspire and intrigue to this day.

The details of the Tuatha Dé Danann's arrival are primarily drawn from ancient Irish texts and sagas. These sources include texts like the "Lebor Gabála Érenn" (The Book of Invasions), which chronicles the various waves of inhabitants in Ireland. While the texts provide a framework for understanding the mythological origins, they also bear the imprint of the cultural and societal contexts in which they were written.

The mythological origins of the Tuatha Dé Danann's arrival are not solely confined to written texts. In fact, much of the rich detail and nuance of the myth was preserved through oral tradition—stories passed down through generations by bards, storytellers, and shamans. This oral tradition ensured that the essence of the Tuatha Dé Danann's story remained alive in the collective memory of the Celtic people.

The Tuatha Dé Danann's arrival resonates with archetypal motifs found in mythologies worldwide. The concept of divine beings descending from a higher realm to bestow their wisdom and gifts upon mortals is a recurring theme in the mythologies of many cultures. This archetype reflects humanity's deep-seated yearning for connection with the transcendent.

One of the intriguing aspects of the Tuatha Dé Danann's arrival is the element of timelessness that envelops their story. The myth blurs the lines between historical reality and spiritual belief, creating a narrative that transcends the constraints of time and invites contemplation on the eternal nature of myth and human imagination.

The mythological origins of the Tuatha Dé Danann's arrival continue to resonate in contemporary times. Their story serves as a reminder of the interconnectedness of myth, history, and cultural identity. The enduring fascination with their arrival underscores the enduring power of storytelling to shape our understanding of the past and our place in the world.

While the details of the Tuatha Dé Danann's arrival may never be fully unraveled, their mystery has given rise to a wealth of speculation and interpretation. Scholars, historians, and enthusiasts continue to explore the nuances of their story, offering various perspectives on the significance of their arrival and the layers of meaning embedded within the myth.

The Tuatha Dé Danann's arrival is more than a static narrative; it is a living myth that evolves with each retelling. As each generation engages with the myth, they contribute new layers of interpretation, cultural context, and personal insight. The myth's ability to adapt and resonate across time underscores its timeless relevance.

The myth and mystery surrounding the Tuatha Dé Danann's arrival in Ireland invite us to explore the intricate interplay between history, folklore, and spiritual belief. Their story represents the merging of the divine with the earthly, the seen with the unseen, and the past with the present. As we delve deeper into this myth, we uncover not only the origins of a legendary people, but also the timeless truths and universal themes that transcend the ages.

Divine Lineage and Connections to Other Mythological Beings

The origins of the Tuatha Dé Danann lie deeply rooted in Celtic mythology, tracing their lineage to the divine realms beyond mortal understanding. According to ancient Celtic beliefs, the Tuatha Dé Danann were descended from the god-like race known as the "Tuatha," meaning "tribes" or "folk," signifying their divine heritage. This connection reflects the reverence and significance placed upon their lineage, marking them as a chosen people with direct connections to the gods.

The Tuatha Dé Danann, often translated as the "the folk of the goddess Danu" or "People of the Goddess Danu," occupy a unique and enduring place in Irish mythology and folklore.

The Tuatha Dé Danann's divine lineage is traced back to their mother goddess, Danu, from whom they take their name. Danu, a goddess associated with fertility, wisdom, and the land, was believed to be the mother of the Tuatha Dé Danann, making her a central figure in their origin myth. This maternal connection highlighted their unique status as the "Children of Danu," reinforcing their divine heritage.

Otherworldly Connections

The Tuatha Dé Danann's origin myth often involves their arrival from the Otherworld, a mystical realm separate from the mortal world. This Otherworldly origin is not unique to the Tuatha Dé Danann alone, as various mythological beings in Celtic traditions were believed to come from or have connections to this ethereal realm. The Otherworld was seen as a place of extraordinary beauty, eternal youth, and advanced knowledge. While the Tuatha Dé Danann have their own unique origin myth, parallels can be drawn between their stories and those of other mythological beings in different cultures. Similarities with the Norse Aesir and Vanir, the Greek gods' emergence from the primordial Chaos, and other worldwide myths of divine beings descending to Earth suggest the universal human need to explain the origins of powerful and extraordinary entities.

Ancestral Echoes in Modern Times
The divine lineage of the Tuatha Dé Danann continues to echo in modern Irish culture. The concept of an ancient lineage connects the people of Ireland to their mythological ancestors, fostering a sense of continuity and pride. In exploring the mythological origins of the Tuatha Dé Danann, we gain insight into their divine lineage, their connections to the Otherworld, and the echoes of their story in modern Irish culture. This chapter sheds light on the foundational beliefs that shaped the identity of the Tuatha Dé Danann as a chosen people with an extraordinary ancestry. Within the intricate tapestry of Irish mythology, the concept of divine bloodlines serves as a common motif that underscores the significance of the Tuatha Dé Danann's origins. The divine lineage is not just a matter of genealogy but a reflection of their inherent connection to the spiritual and supernatural realms.

Danu and Matrilineal Heritage
The role of the mother goddess Danu in the Tuatha Dé Danann's origin narrative carries profound meaning. Matrilineal heritage was highly respected in many ancient cultures, as it symbolized the cyclical nature of life and the importance of nurturing and continuity. The choice to trace the Tuatha Dé Danann's lineage through Danu adds depth to their story, emphasizing the nurturing aspect of divinity and the interconnectedness of all life. While the Tuatha Dé Danann were undoubtedly divine, their interactions with the mortal world blurred the lines between the earthly and divine realms. These interactions were often mediated by individuals who straddled both worlds, highlighting the interconnectedness of the Tuatha Dé Danann with humanity. This dynamic further reinforces the idea that the divine lineage was not isolated, but intricately woven into the fabric of life itself.

Ancestral Connections in Celtic Beliefs
In Celtic belief systems, the past was not merely a series of events, but an ongoing narrative that influenced the present and the future. Ancestral connections were of paramount importance, as they provided a link to ancient wisdom, insights, and protection. The Tuatha Dé Danann's divine lineage reinforced their role as intermediaries between the mortal realm and the realms beyond. The divine lineage of the Tuatha Dé Danann positioned them as custodians of ancient wisdom and arcane knowledge. This role extended beyond mythological tales to encompass a broader cosmic narrative. Through their divine heritage, the Tuatha

Dé Danann became the bearers of cosmic secrets, shaping their interactions with the mortal world and other mythological beings.

The Eternal Cycle of Life and Death

Celtic beliefs were deeply intertwined with the cycles of nature, life, and death. The divine lineage of the Tuatha Dé Danann mirrored these cycles, highlighting the interconnectedness of all existence. Just as the seasons shifted, and the sun rose and set, the Tuatha Dé Danann's divine origins linked them to the eternal rhythms of the cosmos, reinforcing their role as guardians of balance and harmony. The concept of divine lineage is a thread that weaves its way through the tapestry of the Tuatha Dé Danann's stories, their interactions with other mythological beings, and their lasting impact on Irish culture. Their divine origins, connections to the Otherworld, and ancestral echoes form a narrative tapestry that continues to captivate and inspire those who delve into the world of Irish mythology. Throughout history, the interpretation of the Tuatha Dé Danann's divine lineage has evolved, reflecting shifts in cultural beliefs and scholarly understanding. This evolution underscores the adaptability and enduring appeal of these myths, allowing them to remain relevant in different contexts.

Relevance and Reflection

The exploration of the Tuatha Dé Danann's divine lineage invites us to reflect on our own connections to the past, the cosmos, and the mysteries of existence. Their story serves as a mirror that reflects the enduring human quest to understand our origins, our place in the universe, and our relationship with the divine.

In delving into the mythological origins of the Tuatha Dé Danann, we uncover layers of meaning that reveal their divine lineage as a bridge between worlds, a source of cosmic wisdom, and a testament to the eternal cycles of life and death. This lineage is more than a genealogical record; it is a beacon that guides us through the labyrinth of myth and offers insights into the heart of the human experience.

The Tuatha Dé Danann, Aos Sí, and Divine Castes

In the intricate tapestry of Celtic mythology, the Tuatha Dé Danann and the Aos Sí emerge as enigmatic beings who have intrigued scholars and storytellers alike. While early literature occasionally draws distinctions between these two entities, a prevailing notion suggests that they are essentially the same race. The term "Tuatha Dé Danann" stands as the formal and somewhat "literary" name, while "Aos Sí" carries a more familiar and colloquial connotation, symbolizing an evolution from one to the other. The notion, proposed by a minority of contemporary scholars, that the Tuatha Dé and Aos Sí once represented distinct tiers or classes of deities in the pre-Christian pantheon, with echoes of this stratification still present in the literary tradition, remains largely unproven. However, the mythological texts do offer tantalizing glimpses into this complex realm. References to "Déithe agus Andéithe" (Old Irish: "dé ocus andé")—literally "Gods and Un-Gods"—amongst the Tuatha Dé and Aos Sí add a layer of intrigue. Scribes, in their Latin commentaries, explain that the Déithe were their gods, while the Andéithe were their "husbandmen" or commoners, lending credence to the theory and hinting at profound layers of thought behind the nature of the Tuatha Dé.

The relationship between the Tuatha Dé and the Aos Sí bears some resemblance to the more uncertain interplay between gods, particularly the Vanir, and the Alver (Elves) in the mythological traditions of Germanic peoples, including Scandinavians and the English. Modern scholarly consensus leans towards viewing the Vanir as a lower or secondary group of gods in the Icelandic and Scano-Germanic pantheon, with the Æser representing the higher or superior tier. The Vanir appear to have had closer ties to agriculture, fertility, and the natural world, much like the Alver, the debated elfin race of the Germanic world. Many scholars posit that the Vanir and Alver were either identical or originally so. References in later texts to "Light Elves," "Dark Elves," and "Black Elves" in the Eddas—the primary mythological cycle of early Icelandic literature—likely represent contemporary misunderstandings. "Light Elves" are essentially the Alver (Vanir), while "Dark" and "Black Elves" equate to the Dvergar or "Dwarves," who may, in turn, have connections with the Jotne or "Giants," the traditional foes of the gods.

The Tuatha Dé Danann/Aos Sí and the Æser/Vanir/Alver can be regarded as loose analogs of each other, a comparison that can be further dissected into the Aos Sí on one side and the Vanir/Alver on the other. Given the shared Indo-European roots and geographical proximity of Celtic and Germanic peoples, it's not surprising that their mythological traditions exhibit striking similarities. However, one should exercise caution in stretching these comparative parallels too far, as unique facets of language, culture, religion, geography, and history also contribute to significant differences.

In the intricate mosaic of Celtic and Germanic mythologies, these divine castes provide intriguing glimpses into the ancient beliefs and narratives of Europe's largest cultural regions, reminding us of the rich tapestry of human imagination and storytelling that continues to captivate us to this day.

Tuatha Dé Danann and the Belief in Fairies
In the heart of Ireland, where emerald landscapes meet mist-shrouded hills, the ethereal veil between the mortal world and the mystical Otherworld grows thin. It is within this realm of mist and mystery that the stories of the Tuatha Dé Danann and the belief in fairies intertwine—a tapestry woven with threads of myth, folklore, and enchantment. The Tuatha Dé Danann, often referred to as gods and goddesses, descended from the heavens to Ireland. Their arrival was marked by otherworldly magic, a shimmering presence that inspired awe and reverence. These divine beings were masters of art, craftsmanship, and arcane knowledge, and their stories became the foundation of Irish mythology. Legends tell of their epic battles against the Fomorians, mythic sea creatures embodying chaos and darkness. The Tuatha Dé Danann's victory cemented their place as rulers of Ireland, but their story did not end there. Their influence extended beyond mere tales; it was woven into the very fabric of the land.

Folklore: The Transformation into Fairies
As centuries passed, the Tuatha Dé Danann transitioned from divine beings to the fairies of folklore. They stepped from the pages of mythology into the realm of folk belief, becoming entities that dwelled in hills, forests, and meadows—places where the natural and supernatural coexisted. The term "fairies" was applied to a diverse range of beings, each with its own quirks and tendencies.

The transition from gods to fairies marked a transformation of their significance. They were no longer distant and unapproachable deities; they became part of the everyday world, influencing the lives of mortals in myriad ways. Fairies were believed to possess magical abilities, and their interactions with humans often resulted in blessings, misfortune, or the forging of unbreakable pacts. Central to the belief in fairies was the concept of a thin veil separating the mortal realm from the Otherworld—a realm inhabited by the Tuatha Dé Danann. This Otherworld was a place of eternal beauty, where time flowed differently and magic danced in every glimmer of light. The fairies, as denizens of this realm, were both accessible and elusive, visible and hidden.

Folklore spoke of the importance of showing respect to these beings, as they were capable of bestowing blessings or wreaking havoc upon those who crossed their paths. Rituals were performed, offerings were left, and spaces were left undisturbed to avoid offending the fairies. The stories of misfortunes befalling those who disturbed fairy mounds served as a cautionary reminder of the potency of these magical creatures. In the modern context, the legacy of the Tuatha Dé Danann and the belief in fairies remain intertwined with Irish culture. Folklore and myth have become part of the collective identity, celebrated through storytelling, art, literature, and even tourism. The charm of fairies has not faded; they are embraced as a symbol of the enchantment that resides in the Irish landscape. Fairy mounds, or "raths," dot the countryside, carrying echoes of the Tuatha Dé Danann's presence. Celebrations like Bealtaine and Samhain harken back to ancient times when the veil between worlds was believed to be thinnest. The stories of the fairies continue to captivate hearts and minds, reminding us that within the mundane lies the potential for magic.

In essence, the relationship between the Tuatha Dé Danann and the belief in fairies is a testament to the enduring power of myth and folklore. It is a connection that bridges past and present, infusing the Irish landscape with a sense of wonder and mystery—a reminder that even in the modern age, the realms of magic and imagination are never truly out of reach.

Chapter 2
The Divine Pantheon

The Tuatha Dé Danann are a captivating ensemble of divine beings deeply rooted in the rich tapestry of Irish mythology. Within this pantheon, several figures emerge as luminous stars, their stories weaving a complex web of intrigue, heroism, and mysticism. By delving into these well-known members, we embark on a journey through the intricate lore that defines the essence of the Tuatha Dé Danann.

These figures, devoid of formal titles for now, form the nucleus of a captivating saga. Their narratives transcend the mundane and embrace realms of magic and wonder where battles are waged with enchanted weapons, and wisdom flows like an eternal river. Through them, the very essence of Irish mythology is unveiled, illuminated by the timeless stories that have been passed down through generations.

Each member carries a unique mantle, a domain of influence, and a tapestry of interwoven tales that together paint a vivid picture of the Tuatha Dé Danann. Their legends reverberate through the ages, where gods and mortals coexist, and the lines between reality and the Otherworld blur. The ethereal veil of this mystic realm is pierced by their presence, and as we explore their stories, we step into a world where divine power and human destiny intertwine.

The narratives that follow will illuminate these renowned members, their roles, and their enduring significance within the mythology of the Tuatha Dé Danann. Each chapter will unveil the layers of their tales, and as we journey through this mythical tapestry, we shall uncover the profound connections and captivating stories that define this enigmatic pantheon.

Here are some of the key members:

Nuada: The Silver-Armed King

In the tapestry of Irish mythology, Nuada Airgetlám stands out as a pivotal figure within the Tuatha Dé Danann. Known as the king with the silver arm, Nuada's journey is one of leadership, sacrifice, and transformation. His silver arm, forged from both craftsmanship and magic, serves as an enduring symbol of his resilience and unwavering commitment to his people.

The Loss and Consequence Nuada's narrative begins with a fierce battle against the Fir Bolg, a rival group of mythological beings. During this confrontation, Nuada tragically loses his right hand, rendering him ineligible to continue as the king, as tradition dictates that a ruler must be physically perfect. This pivotal event forces the Tuatha Dé Danann to confront a challenging dilemma: How can they maintain their leadership while adhering to their ancient customs?

Dian Cecht's Ingenious Solution The solution comes in the form of Dian Cecht, the skilled physician of the Tuatha Dé Danann. Driven by his commitment to his people and his mastery of healing arts, Dian Cecht takes on the formidable task of crafting a replacement for Nuada's lost hand. With the assistance of his son Miach, Dian Cecht constructs a remarkable and functional silver arm for Nuada, restoring his physical integrity and thereby his kingship.

Myth of Nuada's silver arm

The Symbolic Power of the Silver Arm Beyond its practical purpose, Nuada's silver arm holds profound symbolic significance. It represents not only the fusion of advanced craftsmanship and magical prowess, but also the notion that true leadership transcends physical perfection. Nuada's acceptance of the silver arm reflects his understanding that leadership is a complex blend of strength, wisdom, and adaptability. The arm symbolizes his determination to continue guiding his people, even in the face of adversity. His silver arm becomes an emblem of leadership, determination, and the capacity to overcome challenges. His story is a source of inspiration for future generations, illustrating that true leadership is not confined to physical attributes, but rather rooted in the strength of character and the ability to make difficult choices for the greater good. The myth of Nuada's silver arm continues to resonate in modern times. It serves as a reminder that leaders can emerge from unexpected circumstances, that resilience is a powerful trait, and that sacrifices made for the collective welfare can leave an indelible mark on history. Nuada's silver arm, once a solution to a crisis of kingship, now stands as a timeless symbol of leadership's complexities and the enduring legacy of the Tuatha Dé Danann. His journey captures the essence of mythological tales: a blend of magic and meaning that offers insights into the human condition and the qualities that define remarkable leadership.

Nuada's Leadership and Significance
In the rich tapestry of the Tuatha Dé Danann, Nuada Airgetlám stands as a pivotal figure—a king of both wisdom and resilience, whose presence shapes the very essence of the divine pantheon. This chapter delves into Nuada's remarkable leadership, his struggles, and the profound impact he left on the Tuatha Dé Danann. Nuada's reign as king of the Tuatha Dé Danann was marked by both grandeur and adversity. His name, "Nuada Airgetlám," means "Nuada of the Silver Arm," a testament to the indomitable spirit that defined his leadership. His physical transformation—from a wounded warrior to a king with a silver arm—symbolized his unwavering commitment to his people and the resilience that characterized his rule. Nuada's journey to kingship was not without its trials. In the midst of conflict against the Fir Bolg, he lost his hand in a battle, a devastating injury that seemed to cast doubt on his ability to lead. However, the skilled physician Dian Cecht ingeniously crafted a silver arm to replace what was lost, allowing Nuada to regain his rightful place as king. This replacement arm embodied more than physical restoration; it was a powerful emblem of his ability to overcome adversity and serve as a guiding light for his people.

Symbolism and Role
Nuada's kingship was layered with symbolism. As king, he represented the unity and strength of the Tuatha Dé Danann, guiding them through challenges and fostering a sense of shared purpose. His silver arm, aside from its restorative function, became a symbol of kingship itself—a reminder of his sacrifice for his people and his commitment to the greater good.

Nuada's leadership was tested in the harrowing Battle of Magh Tuireadh, where the Tuatha Dé Danann faced the formidable Fomorians. Nuada's strategic acumen and unwavering courage were pivotal in shaping the outcome of the battle. Despite the battles' challenges, his presence inspired the Tuatha Dé Danann to fight fiercely and defend their realm. The climax of Nuada's story unfolded on the battlefield, where he valiantly fought but ultimately lost his life. His sacrifice was a poignant moment that showcased his selflessness and devotion to his people. As he fell in battle, he passed the mantle of leadership to Lugh Lámhfhada, a skilled and multi-talented god who would carry the torch forward.

Nuada's Enduring Impact
Nuada's legacy transcends his time as king. He left an indelible mark on the Tuatha Dé Danann, becoming a symbol of resilience, sacrifice, and the strength that can arise from adversity. His story continues to resonate in the hearts of those who recount the tales of the Tuatha Dé Danann, reminding them of the unwavering commitment and nobility that define true leadership.

As the divine pantheon of the Tuatha Dé Danann weaves together a tapestry of personalities and stories, Nuada's chapter stands out as a testament to the power of leadership, transformation, and the enduring impact of those who rise above challenges to guide their people toward a brighter future.

Lugh: The Multi-Faceted Hero

Lugh Lámhfhada, often referred to as Lugh of the Long Arm, is a multifaceted and revered god within the Tuatha Dé Danann pantheon. His significance is attributed to his versatile abilities, leadership qualities, and heroic deeds. Let's delve into the detailed exploration of Lugh's roles as a warrior, craftsman, and more.

Lugh's Roles as a Warrior

Lugh is widely known for his prowess as a warrior and a hero. He is celebrated for his exceptional skills in combat, strategy, and leadership on the battlefield.

Battle Tactics and Strategy: Lugh's strategic brilliance earned him a prominent position within the ranks of the Tuatha Dé Danann during the Battle of Magh Tuireadh. He demonstrated a keen understanding of battle tactics, often positioning himself where his skills were most needed.

Slaying of Balor

One of Lugh's most renowned feats was his slaying of Balor of the Evil Eye, a formidable Fomorian leader. Lugh's precise aim with a sling and stone managed to pierce Balor's eye, causing the Fomorian leader's demise. This act of courage and precision turned the tide of the battle and led to the Tuatha Dé Danann's victory. Lugh's tales of heroism extend beyond the battlefield. His stories include rescuing captives, defeating monsters, and contributing to the overall well-being of his people. These tales showcase his multifaceted nature and his commitment to protecting his kin.

Lugh's Roles as a Craftsman and Artisan

Lugh's abilities go beyond warfare; he is also recognized as a skilled craftsman and artisan. His craftsmanship embodies creativity, innovation, and a deep connection to the arts.

Lugh's Spear: Lugh is associated with a magical spear known as the "Slaughterer" or "Lúin." This spear is often depicted as an embodiment of Lugh's divine power and his ability to conquer adversaries. It is said to possess the power to pierce through any defense.

Skills in Metalwork and Craftsmanship: Lugh's expertise is not limited to battle equipment. He is credited with exceptional skills in metalwork, including crafting intricate jewelry and ornaments. These creations reflect his artistic talent and his contribution to the cultural heritage of the Tuatha Dé Danann. Lugh's craftsman roles extend to the realm of culture and knowledge. His association with art, poetry, and music highlights his appreciation for the finer aspects of life. Lugh's influence in promoting cultural expression contributes to his multifaceted persona.

Lugh's Roles as a Leader and Protector

Beyond his specific roles as a warrior and craftsman, Lugh's overarching role within the Tuatha Dé Danann pantheon is that of a leader and protector. Lugh's leadership during the Battle of Magh Tuireadh solidified his reputation as a capable and strategic leader. His ability to unite the Tuatha Dé Danann against the Fomorians showcased his leadership qualities and his dedication to the welfare of his people.

Lugh is often regarded as a guardian figure for the Tuatha Dé Danann. His roles as a warrior and protector align with his responsibility to defend his kin from threats, both external and internal.

Lugh's various roles within the pantheon demonstrate his efforts to cultivate unity among the Tuatha Dé Danann. His influence as a unifying force helps bind the divine community together, fostering cooperation and collective strength. In essence, Lugh Lámhfhada's dynamic roles as a warrior, craftsman, leader, and protector exemplify the complexity of his character within the Tuatha Dé Danann pantheon. His stories resonate with themes of heroism, innovation, and dedication to his people, making him one of the most revered figures in Irish mythology. Lugh, often known as Lugh Lámhfhada or Lugh of the Long Arm, holds a prominent place within the Tuatha Dé Danann pantheon. His multifaceted nature, heroic exploits, and unique attributes make him one of the most revered and complex deities in Irish mythology.

Lugh's Connection to the Sun and his divine attributes

Lugh's connection to the sun is a central aspect of his identity, symbolizing his radiant qualities and multifarious roles within the Tuatha Dé Danann pantheon. As the sun illuminates and sustains, so does Lugh's presence and influence illuminate the realm of myth. Attributes and

Roles Lugh embodies the archetype of the radiant hero, possessing a diverse array of attributes that set him apart as a god of extraordinary talents and skills.

Lugh's proficiency in various crafts, arts, and skills makes him a patron of creativity and innovation. He is known for his mastery in areas such as swordsmanship, spear throwing, poetry, and more. Lugh's talents reflect the importance of skill and excellence within the Tuatha Dé Danann society.

As a god of combat, Lugh takes on the role of a warrior and protector. His associations with warfare align him with the defense of his people against external threats, as seen in his participation in the Battle of Magh Tuireadh against the Fomorians.

Harvest and Fertility

Lugh's connection to the sun extends to his role as a deity associated with harvest and fertility. His life-giving attributes are mirrored in the bountiful harvests that sustain the population.

Lugh is also linked to eloquence and communication, reflected in his ability to engage in compelling speech and persuasion. He's seen as a mediator and diplomat, traits that contribute to his leadership abilities.

Lugh's Role in Mythological Narratives:

Lugh's involvement in significant mythological narratives showcases his dynamic attributes and enduring legacy. Lugh's heroic leadership during the Battle of Magh Tuireadh stands as a testament to his strategic prowess and courage. His pivotal role in leading the Tuatha Dé Danann to victory against the Fomorians solidifies his status as a heroic figure.

Lugh and Celtic Festivals

1. Lughnasadh - The Festival of Lugh: Lughnasadh, also known as Lúnasa or Lammas, is one of the four major seasonal festivals in the Celtic calendar, along with Imbolc, Beltane, and Samhain. It is celebrated on August 1st, roughly halfway between the summer solstice and the autumn equinox. Lughnasadh is named after Lugh, the god of many skills, who presides over this festival.

2. Harvest Celebration: Lughnasadh primarily marks the beginning of the harvest season in Celtic lands. It is a time when the first crops, particularly grains like wheat and barley, are ready for harvesting. The

festival celebrates the bounty of the earth and the hard work of farmers and agricultural communities. This period was crucial for the survival of ancient Celtic societies, and Lughnasadh served as a time to give thanks for the harvest.

3. *Games and Competitions:* Lughnasadh was a time for communal gatherings and festivities. Games and competitions, such as athletic contests, races, and martial arts demonstrations, were common during this festival. These competitions not only provided entertainment, but also allowed individuals to showcase their physical skills and prowess, reflecting Lugh's role as a skilled warrior and athlete.

4. *Arts and Crafts:* Lughnasadh also celebrated the arts and crafts, which were an integral part of Celtic culture. Artisans, bards, and musicians would showcase their talents during the festival. It was a time for storytelling, poetry, music, and the display of intricate craftsmanship. This aspect of the festival pays homage to Lugh's role as a master craftsman and artisan.

5. *Pilgrimages and Rituals:* In addition to the festive and competitive aspects, Lughnasadh had its religious and spiritual significance. People would make pilgrimages to sacred sites, hills, or mountains associated with Lugh, where rituals and ceremonies were held to honor the god and seek his blessings for a bountiful harvest. These rituals often included offerings of the first fruits and grains.

6. *Bonfires and Feasting:* Bonfires were a common feature of Lughnasadh celebrations. These fires were symbolic of the sun's strength and power during the summer months. People would leap over the fires for luck and protection. After the games, competitions, and rituals, a grand feast would follow, featuring the newly harvested crops and other locally sourced foods. This communal feast was a time for sharing, socializing, and strengthening community bonds.

7. *Modern Celebrations*: While Lughnasadh is rooted in ancient Celtic traditions, it continues to be celebrated in modern times, albeit with some adaptations. Many modern pagan and neopagan communities observe Lughnasadh as a time to connect with nature, honor the harvest, and celebrate creativity and skills. It often involves gatherings, feasting, music, and dance, as well as crafting and artistic activities.

The Solar Symbolism: Sun God or Solar Hero?
Lugh's solar symbolism raises questions about whether he is a sun god or a solar hero. While he embodies solar attributes, his multifunctional role expands beyond mere solar worship. Instead, he is a nuanced character whose radiance extends to various realms of life. Lugh's Legacy and Influence Lugh's connection to the sun, his multifarious attributes, and his heroic feats cement his legacy within Irish mythology. His representation as a radiant hero embodies the complexities of leadership, excellence, and resilience, making him an enduring source of inspiration for generations to come.

In summary, Lugh's connection to the sun is a testament to his radiant qualities as a heroic and multi-skilled deity within the Tuatha Dé Danann pantheon. His multifunctional role as a master of skills, protector, and embodiment of solar attributes enriches the tapestry of Irish mythology and reflects the ideals of heroism and leadership.

Brigid: Triple Goddess of Vitality

The Three Aspects of Brigid: Healing, Poetry, and Smithcraft

In the rich tapestry of Irish mythology, the Tuatha Dé Danann stand as luminous figures, their divine essence woven intricately into the fabric of the land's cultural identity. Among these revered deities, Brigid emerges as a particularly captivating and complex goddess, embodying three distinct but interconnected aspects: healing, poetry, and smith craft. This trinity of roles not only underscores Brigid's multifaceted nature but also mirrors the multifarious aspects of life itself, reflecting the harmonious blend of creation, preservation, and transformation.

Brigid, often referred to as Brigid the Healer, holds a nurturing and benevolent presence in the pantheon. Her association with healing extends beyond physical ailments to encompass emotional and spiritual well-being. As the protector of mothers and newborns, she is invoked during childbirth to bestow her blessings of safety and ease. Springs and wells are dedicated to her as sites of healing, where her touch is believed to restore vitality to those who seek solace in her domain. Brigid's ability to mend wounds, both physical and emotional, serves as a poignant reminder of the healing power inherent in the divine and in the cycles of life.

Brigid's second facet, that of the muse and patroness of poetry, underscores the profound relationship between creativity and the divine. She is venerated as the source of inspiration, her presence felt in the lyrical verses that flow from bards' lips and the imagery woven into tales of enchantment. As the protector of the spoken word, she bestows the gift of eloquence upon storytellers, empowering them to captivate audiences and preserve the wisdom of generations. Brigid's association with poetry not only elevates the arts but also underscores the significance of communication in forging connections and transmitting cultural heritage.

The third aspect of Brigid's triadic nature, that of the smith, embodies the transformative power inherent in creation. Through her patronage of smithcraft, Brigid guides the hands of artisans who forge metals into intricate works of art and utility. The forge becomes a sacred space, symbolizing the alchemical process of change and renewal. In myth, Brigid's divine presence is said to bless the fires of the forge, infusing the crafted objects with her essence. This confluence of fire and creativity reflects the interconnectedness of the divine with human endeavors, reminding us of our role as co-creators in the world.

The intertwining of these three aspects of Brigid creates a vivid mosaic that captures the essence of life itself. As a healing goddess, she reminds us of the restorative power of compassion and care, sustaining the circle of life. Her role as a patroness of poetry highlights the transcendent nature of creativity, drawing the divine into the realm of human expression. Finally, as a goddess of smith craft, she symbolizes transformation, forging connections between the ethereal and the tangible.

The divine pantheon of the Tuatha Dé Danann is a realm of intricate layers, each deity a prism refracting the myriad facets of existence. Among them, Brigid shines as a luminary, embodying the essence of healing, poetry, and smith craft. Through her, we are reminded of the interconnectedness of life's diverse threads and the perpetual dance between creation, preservation, and transformation. Just as Brigid's triadic nature harmonizes these aspects, so too does she harmonize the tapestry of Irish mythology, weaving a narrative that celebrates the divine within the earthly realm.

Brigid: The Triple Goddess of Fertility
Poetry, and Healing Brigid's triple aspect reflects the multifaceted nature of life. Her connection to fertility aligns with festivals celebrating life's regenerative cycles. Imbolc, the festival marking the return of spring, carries her presence, symbolizing the emergence of life from the dormant winter. Brigid's link to poetry is a reminder of the potency of language and artistic expression, key components of festivals that seek to convey meaning through creativity. As a healer, she accentuates the

significance of wellness in Celtic culture, a theme echoing in festivals that blend spirituality with physical well-being.

Christianization of Brigid

With the spread of Christianity in Ireland, Brigid was transformed into Saint Brigid, who shares many attributes with her pagan counterpart. This Christianized version of Brigid is known as one of the patron saints of Ireland and is associated with acts of charity, hospitality, and the foundation of religious institutions, such as the Kildare Abbey, where a sacred flame was tended in her honor.

Imbolc, celebrated on February 1st or 2nd, is the primary festival dedicated to Brigid. It marks the midway point between the winter solstice and the spring equinox, symbolizing the gradual return of warmth and light to the world. During this festival, people would light bonfires, make offerings to Brigid, and engage in purification rituals, symbolizing the cleansing and renewing power of fire.

Symbols and Iconography:

Brigid is often represented with several symbols, including:

- The Triple Spiral: This symbolizes her triple aspect as a goddess of healing, poetry, and smith craft.
- The Flame: Fire is a central element associated with Brigid, symbolizing her transformative and purifying qualities.
- The Cross of Brigid (Brigid's Cross): This woven straw or reed cross is a protective talisman, often placed above doorways or in homes to invoke her blessings and ward off evil.

Modern Relevance

Brigid continues to be a significant figure in modern Celtic and pagan spirituality. Many people celebrate Imbolc and honor Brigid's triadic aspects by incorporating her symbols and rituals into their practices. She is seen as a source of inspiration, creativity, and healing, making her a beloved and enduring figure in contemporary spirituality. In conclusion, Brigid, the Triple Goddess of Fertility, is a captivating and enduring figure in Celtic mythology and folklore. Her triadic nature reflects the interconnectedness of healing, creativity, and craftsmanship, making her a symbol of renewal and abundance. Whether as a pagan goddess or a Christian saint, Brigid remains a beloved and influential figure in Irish and Celtic culture, embodying the timeless qualities of fertility, inspiration, and protection.

Dagda: The All-Father of Abundance

Dagda's Magical Club and Cauldron of Plenty

In the rich tapestry of Irish mythology, the Tuatha Dé Danann stand as a remarkable assembly of divine beings, each with their unique attributes and contributions. Among them, the enigmatic Dagda, often referred to as the "good god," commands attention with his powerful and iconic magical items - the enchanted club and the cauldron of plenty. These artifacts, laden with symbolism and significance, provide a profound glimpse into Dagda's character, his role as a god of abundance, and his impact on the mythological landscape.

Dagda: The "Good God" of Abundance Before delving into the intricacies of his artifacts, it is vital to understand Dagda's role in Celtic mythology. As a deity embodying abundance, the fertility of the land, and the cyclical nature of life, Dagda transcends traditional conceptions of gods. His name itself, meaning "good god," reflects his benevolent nature and his capacity to bestow nourishment, prosperity, and wisdom upon his people.

The Magical Club: A Symbol of Power and Command

At the heart of Dagda's divine arsenal lies his formidable club, a symbol of his authority and might. This massive cudgel, sometimes called "the club of the battles," possesses a unique trait: one end can kill, while the other end can resurrect. This duality embodies the cycle of life and death, reflecting the interconnectedness of all things. Dagda's club goes beyond brute force; it symbolizes balanced strength and the use of power for both creation and protection. In mythological accounts, he employs the club to clear forests and plains, making space for cultivation. This attribute underlines his role in fostering fertility and growth, and it reveals his deep connection to the land.

The Cauldron of Plenty

A Source of Sustenance and Renewal Adjacent to Dagda's club in significance is the mystical cauldron of plenty. This vessel, imbued with magic, has the power to provide an endless bounty of food. The cauldron embodies themes of generosity, abundance, and renewal, echoing the themes of fertility and the perpetual cycle of life. The cauldron serves as a metaphorical representation of Dagda's character - a provider who ensures that his people never go hungry. The cauldron's generosity ties into the concept of community, as Dagda embodies the nurturing father figure, taking care of his people's physical and spiritual needs.

Origins and Characteristics:
The Cauldron of Plenty is often depicted as a large, magical cauldron with the ability to produce an endless supply of food. This food is said to be nourishing and satisfying, capable of providing sustenance for all who partake of it. The cauldron is described as bottomless, and no matter how much food is taken from it, it never empties. This attribute makes it a symbol of abundance and fertility. In one of the most famous myths involving the Cauldron of Plenty, Dagda is said to own the cauldron and uses it to feed his people during times of need. In this story, he invites all the Tuatha Dé Danann to a feast, where they gather around the cauldron and are fed to their heart's content. This cauldron exemplifies the idea of plenty and the importance of communal sharing and hospitality in Celtic culture.

Symbolism and Themes
The Cauldron of Plenty holds several symbolic meanings and themes in Celtic mythology and beyond:

- Abundance and Fertility: The cauldron represents the concept of fertility and abundance in Celtic culture. It is a symbol of the land's fertility and its ability to provide for its people.
- Nourishment and Sustenance: The food produced by the cauldron is not just physical sustenance but also represents emotional and spiritual nourishment. It embodies the idea of nurturing and caring for the community.
- Rebirth and Regeneration: The Cauldron of Plenty is often associated with the idea of rebirth and regeneration. Its never-ending food supply can be seen as a metaphor for the cyclical nature of life and death.
- Community and Hospitality: The cauldron emphasizes the importance of community and hospitality in Celtic culture. It highlights the notion of sharing resources and taking care of one another.

- Divine Power: The cauldron's magical properties are a testament to the supernatural elements present in Celtic mythology. It showcases the gods' ability to manipulate the natural world.

Influence on Modern Culture

The Cauldron of Plenty and the stories surrounding it continue to influence modern culture, particularly in Ireland and other Celtic regions. It is a symbol of generosity, prosperity, and the interconnectedness of individuals within a community. This symbolism is often incorporated into modern celebrations, art, and literature. The magical club and the cauldron of plenty encapsulate Dagda's multifaceted nature and his impact on the Tuatha Dé Danann's mythology. The duality of the club reflects the dual aspects of life and death, creation and destruction, while the cauldron represents the sustaining force of nature and the divine gift of abundance. Together, these artifacts create a synergy that embodies the essence of Dagda - a deity of generosity, strength, and balanced power.

Dagda's legacy endures, not only in the mythological tales but also in their resonances through time. His attributes are deeply embedded in Irish culture and its connections to the land and community. As we contemplate Dagda's magical club and cauldron of plenty, we unearth layers of symbolism that enrich our understanding of the complex world of the Tuatha Dé Danann, offering a glimpse into the heart of a deity who embodies the essential elements of sustenance, renewal, and benevolence.

His Influence on Life and Death in Irish Mythology

In the rich tapestry of Irish mythology, the Tuatha Dé Danann stand as a remarkable pantheon of gods and goddesses, each embodying distinct attributes and roles. Among them, the enigmatic figure of Dagda emerges as a central deity with profound influence over the realms of life and death. As the "good god" of abundance and magic, Dagda's multifaceted character reverberates through myths, symbolizing themes of fertility, power, and cosmic balance. Dagda's significance in the divine pantheon lies in his embodiment of life's essential aspects. His portrayal encompasses numerous attributes, such as his mighty club, a symbol of strength, and his magical cauldron, which serves as a vessel of inexhaustible abundance. His harp, capable of playing soothing or devastating melodies, further underscores his dual nature as a benevolent protector and an enforcer of justice.

Fertility and Abundance
Dagda's association with fertility intertwines with his portrayal as a divine ancestor and provider. His cauldron exemplifies this aspect, as it bestows unending sustenance upon those who gather around it. This imagery of abundance aligns with his role as a nurturing deity, ensuring the prosperity of his people and the land. By overseeing the cycles of growth and harvest, Dagda becomes a symbol of the life-giving forces of the natural world. Dagda's influence extends beyond the boundaries of the mortal realm into the realm of death. His pivotal role in mediating life and death is embodied in his connection to the River Unius, a threshold between the worlds. This representation aligns with the cyclical worldview of Celtic mythology, where life and death are interconnected stages of existence. In this capacity, Dagda takes on a dual role as a guardian of life and as a guide for souls in the transition to the Otherworld.

Harmony and Cosmic Balance
Dagda's significance also extends to the cosmic balance that governs the universe. His presence and attributes reflect the harmonious coexistence of opposites: life and death, creation and destruction. This interplay underscores the interconnectedness of all things and emphasizes the cyclical nature of existence. Dagda, with his ability to both create and dismantle, embodies the equilibrium necessary for the universe's continual renewal. Dagda's role as a divine judge and enforcer of justice is evident in his harp's music, which can either soothe or cause chaos. His sense of fairness and his role in maintaining cosmic order extend to his representation as a moral compass. In this capacity, he ensures that equilibrium is upheld not only in the natural world but also in the realms of ethics and behavior. Dagda's influence on life and death resonates through generations, as his myths continue to captivate and inspire. Modern interpretations recognize his representation of life's complexities and the multifaceted nature of existence. His embodiment of cosmic balance, fertility, and justice offers valuable insights into the delicate interplay of forces that shape the world.

Dagda's significance in the Irish pantheon goes beyond being a mere deity; he is a living embodiment of the intricate relationships between life and death, creation and dissolution. His influence pervades every aspect of existence, from the growth of crops to the transitions of souls. Through his attributes and roles, Dagda remains a timeless symbol of the enduring cycles that underpin Irish mythology and the cosmos itself.

Ogma: Master of Eloquence

Ogma's Role as a Champion and Scholar

Ogma emerges as a multifaceted deity, revered for his dual roles as a fearless champion and a wise scholar. Ogma's character encapsulates the intricate blend of strength and intellect that defines the Tuatha Dé Danann, offering a captivating exploration into his contributions to both warfare and knowledge. Ogma's prominent role as a champion is perhaps best exemplified by his prowess on the battlefield. As a warrior god, he embodies the spirit of martial excellence and valor, representing the indomitable strength and courage of the Tuatha Dé Danann. Ogma's feats of arms in various mythological accounts underscore his role as a fierce defender of his people. His skill in combat is not only a testament to his own might but also symbolizes the Tuatha Dé Danann's resilience against adversarial forces.

Scholarly Pursuits and Intellectual Eminence

Ogma's significance transcends his martial valor, as he also holds a distinct place as a scholar and linguist within the Tuatha Dé Danann pantheon. His portrayal as a scholar underscores the Tuatha Dé Danann's veneration for knowledge and intellectual pursuits. Ogma's association with the invention of the Ogham script—an ancient writing system that used notches and lines to represent sounds—highlights his contributions to language and communication, making him a patron of eloquence, poetry, and wisdom.

The Invention of Ogham Script and Its Significance

The Tuatha Dé Danann posses a rich tapestry of attributes and roles that shape their significance within the Celtic folklore. Among their myriad talents, the creation of the Ogham script stands out as a remarkable achievement that highlights their connection to communication, wisdom, and the written word. Ogham, an ancient script developed by the Tuatha Dé Danann, stands as a testament to their commitment to the preservation of knowledge and the art of communication. This script, consisting of a series of notches and lines carved onto stone, wood, or other surfaces, is renowned for its enigmatic appearance and deep historical roots. Ogham is often associated with Ogma, the deity responsible for its creation and the embodiment of eloquence and expression. Ogma, esteemed for his unparalleled eloquence and linguistic mastery, holds a vital role in the invention of Ogham. As the god of communication and expression, his involvement in creating a script that serves as a written form of language is deeply fitting. According to myth, Ogma devised the Ogham script as a way to preserve and transmit knowledge, allowing individuals to inscribe their thoughts onto various mediums, transcending the boundaries of oral tradition.

The invention of the Ogham script by Ogma and its integration into Celtic culture holds significant implications. Firstly, Ogham enabled the Tuatha Dé Danann and other inhabitants of ancient Ireland to document their wisdom, traditions, and stories, transcending the constraints of time and memory. It became a vehicle through which knowledge could be disseminated across generations, fostering a sense of cultural continuity. Furthermore, the Ogham script is deeply connected to the land itself. Each character in the Ogham alphabet is associated with a specific tree, aligning the script with the natural world. This interweaving of language and nature exemplifies the Tuatha Dé Danann's reverence for the environment and their understanding of the intrinsic link between language, culture, and the physical world.

The legacy of the Ogham script endures to this day. Its presence is etched into ancient stones and carvings, preserving glimpses of ancient Celtic thought and history. Additionally, the Ogham script continues to captivate modern scholars, artists, and enthusiasts, sparking discussions about its origins, interpretation, and impact. Its symbolism as a bridge between the ethereal and the tangible serves as a reminder of the Tuatha Dé Danann's enduring influence on the fabric of Irish culture.

In summary, the invention of the Ogham script by the Tuatha Dé Danann, with the guidance of Ogma, encapsulates their multifaceted abilities and their commitment to preserving wisdom and knowledge. This script, with its enigmatic lines and profound connection to the land, serves as a lasting testament to the divine pantheon's influence on communication, culture, and the enduring allure of Irish mythology. The Ogham script stands as a unique embodiment of the Tuatha Dé Danann's legacy, encapsulating their role as bearers of wisdom and keepers of tradition.

Ogma's Battle and Weaponry
One of the most famous narratives that showcases Ogma's martial prowess is his participation in the Battle of Magh Tuireadh, a monumental clash between the Tuatha Dé Danann and the formidable Fomorians. In this battle, Ogma's mighty blows and fearless demeanor played a vital role in securing victory for his people. His preferred weapon, the Gáe Bulg—a formidable spear capable of delivering fatal wounds—became an emblem of his might and tactical acumen. This weapon, attributed to him, exemplifies the divine weaponry wielded by the Tuatha Dé Danann and is emblematic of Ogma's martial skill.

Ogma's dual roles as a champion and scholar highlight the harmonious complexity of the Tuatha Dé Danann pantheon. His embodiment of both physical might and intellectual brilliance showcases the interconnectedness of strength and wisdom, demonstrating that these qualities are not mutually exclusive. Ogma's persona underscores the pantheon's diverse attributes, echoing the multifaceted nature of the divine beings that populate Irish mythology. Ogma's legacy endures through the Ogham script, which remains a testament to his enduring influence. As a warrior god and scholar, Ogma bridges the realms of martial prowess and intellectual depth, embodying the essence of the Tuatha Dé Danann's intricate mythology. His presence reminds us that the divine pantheon, much like life itself, thrives on balance, diversity, and the intertwining of seemingly disparate qualities.

Ogma's role as a champion and scholar within the Tuatha Dé Danann pantheon exemplifies the multifaceted nature of these divine beings. His dual personas of a valiant warrior and an erudite scholar showcase the harmony between strength and intellect, contributing to the rich tapestry of Irish mythology. Ogma's legacy continues to captivate our imagination, serving as a reminder of the profound complexity and diversity inherent in both the divine and mortal realms.

Aengus: God of Love and Youth

Aengus's Associations with Romance and Beauty

Aengus Mac Og emerges as a deity adorned with the resplendent hues of romance and beauty. Aengus, often referred to as Aengus the Young or Aengus of the Brugh, encapsulates the essence of passion, love, and aesthetic splendor within the divine pantheon. Aengus Mac Og, a son of the Dagda, takes his place as a god of prominence within the Tuatha Dé Danann. His name resonates with lyrical cadence, evoking a sense of youthful energy and allure. Often associated with youthfulness, Aengus stands as a symbol of perpetual beauty and vitality, transcending the boundaries of time. The name "Mac Og" itself translates to "Son of Youth," a moniker that encapsulates his essence.

The Mists of Love

Aengus's most celebrated role lies within the realm of love and romance. His enchanting tale of unrequited love for Caer Ibormeith "the goddess of sleep and dreams" casts a spell upon the hearts of those who hear it. Aengus's pursuit of Caer, a swan maiden, encapsulates the longing and devotion characteristic of romantic narratives. This pursuit is emblematic of the intricate dance between the mortal and the divine, as Aengus's journey to win Caer's affection involves traversing both the ethereal and earthly realms.

His Quest for the Dream Girl, Caer Ibormeith

Aengus's quest for Caer Ibormeith is a tale of unparalleled devotion and determination. Caer, a swan maiden, captures Aengus's heart in a dream. He is so smitten that he embarks on a relentless pursuit to find her in the mortal realm. Aengus learns that Caer transforms into a swan by day and a beautiful woman by night. He discovers that she resides on a mystical lake surrounded by 150 other swan maidens. Determined to be reunited with his dream girl, Aengus sets out on a journey fraught with challenges.

The story of Aengus and Caer delves into the themes of transformation and perseverance. Aengus's unyielding commitment to finding Caer speaks to the depth of his love and his willingness to undergo trials to be with her. His ability to navigate between the mortal world and the realm of swan maidens showcases the blurring of boundaries between reality and the magical Otherworld, a recurring theme in Irish mythology.

Aengus's father, the Dagda, intervenes to aid his son in his quest for Caer. The Dagda arranges for Aengus to meet Caer at the exact moment of her transformation from swan to woman. Aengus's love and determination touch Caer's heart, and she willingly joins him in a union that mirrors the harmony of nature.

Love Beyond Boundaries

The story of Aengus and Caer epitomizes the idea of love transcending boundaries. Aengus's unwavering pursuit of Caer underscores the belief that love has the power to bridge gaps between different realms and identities. Their love story highlights the intertwining of mortal and divine destinies, reflecting the complexity and beauty of relationships. The narrative of Aengus and Caer Ibormeith resonates as a testament to the enduring nature of love, the transformative power of devotion, and the interconnectedness of mortal and divine realms. Aengus's quest for his dream girl embodies the ideals of youth, beauty, and the profound emotions that inspire human hearts. As a figure within the Tuatha Dé Danann pantheon, Aengus reminds us of the ethereal nature of love and its ability to transcend both time and reality, weaving a tapestry of enchantment that captivates and endures through the ages. Aengus's dwelling, the Brugh na Bóinne, further embellishes his association with the enchanting and the beautiful. This Otherworldly abode, nestled within the landscape of the Boyne Valley, is described as a realm where time flows differently.

Aengus's connection to the Brugh mirrors his capacity to transport mortals and deities alike to a dreamscape suffused with aesthetic charm. This domain becomes a setting where the boundaries between reality and the ethereal blur, fostering an environment ripe for the blooming of passions.

The Harp of Emotions

Intricately woven into Aengus's narrative is the tale of his harp that plays melodies resonating with the emotional spectrum. The strings of this harp embody the very essence of beauty, as its notes evoke feelings of love, sorrow, joy, and longing. The harmony created by the harp signifies the interconnectedness of emotions and the beauty they bring to life's tapestry. Aengus's influence extends to the celebration of Imbolc, a festival marking the arrival of spring. Imbolc, often associated with the goddess Brigid, aligns harmoniously with Aengus's attributes of youth and beauty. As winter's grasp begins to loosen, Aengus's presence infuses the season with a sense of renewal, encouraging the emergence of life's vibrant hues. Aengus Mac Og's associations with romance and beauty resonate not only within the mythological narratives but also within the human experience. His portrayal mirrors the profound yearning for love, passion, and aesthetic appreciation that resides deep within the human soul. Through Aengus's tales, the Tuatha Dé Danann beckon mortals to embrace the enchanting qualities that make life's journey a tapestry of emotions and experiences.

Within the captivating assembly of the Tuatha Dé Danann's divine pantheon, Aengus Mac Og stands as a beacon of romance and beauty. His role in the mythology weaves a tapestry that intertwines the ethereal and the earthly, the longing and the fulfillment, and the dreamlike with the tangible. Through Aengus's stories, the essence of love and beauty continues to echo across the ages, reminding us of the enduring power of the heart's desires and the exquisite allure of the world that surrounds us.

Manannán mac Lir: Lord of the Sea and Otherworld

Manannán's Connection to the Sea and Navigation

Manannán mac Lir emerges as a prominent figure with a profound association to the sea and navigation. His status as a sea god not only reflects his role in the divine pantheon but also offers insights into the significance of the sea in Celtic culture, the symbolism surrounding water, and the realm of the Otherworld. Manannán mac Lir is a son of Lir, another sea deity, and his lineage underscores his close connection to the maritime realm. Often depicted as a master of the seas, Manannán's name itself translates to "Son of Lir," reinforcing his divine ancestry and his role as a guardian of the oceans and waterways. This lineage places him at the intersection of both human and divine domains, representing a bridge between mortal sailors and the divine forces governing the tides.

Guardian of the Waters

Navigating the Seas: Manannán's significance is most pronounced in his role as a guardian and guide for sailors navigating the treacherous waters. Mythological narratives often depict him aiding mariners in times of need, ensuring safe passage through stormy seas and unfamiliar currents. This portrayal highlights the reverence sailors held for him, acknowledging his authority over the unpredictable waters and their reliance on his benevolence. Manannán's connection to the sea extends beyond mere navigation. The sea, in Celtic culture, is often regarded as a liminal space, a boundary between the mortal world and the mystical Otherworld. This notion aligns with the belief that the Tuatha Dé Danann hail from the Otherworld and possess knowledge and powers inaccessible to humans. Manannán's dominion over the sea thus reinforces his role as a bridge between these two realms, facilitating the exchange of wisdom, magic, and protection.

His role as a guardian of the Otherworldly realms
Manannán mac Lir's role as a guardian of the Otherworldly realms is a profound and intricate aspect of Celtic mythology. The connection between Manannán and the Otherworld is not a mere footnote in the annals of folklore; it is woven into the very fabric of his being and manifests in myriad myths and stories. At the heart of his mystical prowess lies his magnificent steed, Enbarr. This remarkable horse possesses the extraordinary ability to traverse both land and sea, symbolizing the fluidity between realities. Enbarr's hooves touch not just earthly soil but also the hidden depths of the ocean, effortlessly bridging the gap between the mundane and the supernatural. Manannán's association with such a magical companion highlights his own ethereal nature and his unique role as a conduit between worlds.

Perhaps the most iconic emblem of Manannán's connection to the Otherworld is his ever-shifting cloak, often depicted as an enigmatic mist. This cloak, which grants him the power of invisibility, serves as a poignant symbol of his ethereal essence. Just as the mist conceals and reveals, Manannán's role is to guide and protect, to veil the mystical from mortal eyes, and to unveil it when the time is right. In this, he underscores his pivotal role in facilitating communication and interaction between the mortal and divine realms, serving as a bridge that transcends the boundaries of existence. The cultural significance of Manannán extends far beyond the realm of myth. Coastal communities, intimately tied to the sea for sustenance and trade, held him in the highest esteem. They offered heartfelt prayers and humble offerings to seek his protection and benevolence. The symbolism of the sea as both a source of life and a realm of profound mystery and challenge further amplifies Manannán's significance. He embodies the duality of the ocean—the giver of life's bounty and the harbinger of storms and peril.
In the intricate tapestry of Irish mythology, Manannán mac Lir emerges as a central figure in the divine pantheon, intricately linked to the sea and navigation. His multifaceted role as guardian, guide, and bridge between realms speaks to the reverence for water's dual nature as both a life-giver and an enigma. Through Manannán's profound connection to the sea, we gain profound insights into the spiritual significance of maritime endeavors, the tantalizing mysteries of the Otherworld, and the enduring cultural legacy of Celtic beliefs.

Sailors of old and those who still navigate the seas today continue to look to Manannán for safe passage. His legacy endures, navigating the currents of history and imagination, a guardian of the Otherworldly realms and a timeless symbol of the intertwined relationship between humanity, the sea, and the mysteries that lie beyond.

Dian Cecht: Master Healer and Physician

Dian Cecht's Healing Skills and Nuada's Silver Arm

Dian Cecht's exceptional healing skills and Nuada's iconic silver arm stand out as emblematic symbols of resilience, sacrifice, and the extraordinary power wielded by the divine beings.

Dian Cecht emerges as a pivotal figure in the Divine Pantheon of the Tuatha Dé Danann, celebrated for his unparalleled mastery of healing arts. He embodies the archetype of the skilled physician and stands as a symbol of rejuvenation, restoration, and the harmonious balance between life and death. His influence is rooted not only in his ability to mend physical wounds, but also in the compassionate care he offers to those in need.

In the intricate web of Irish mythology, Dian Cecht's prominence is particularly evident in his instrumental role in crafting Nuada's silver arm. This feat of artistry and magic symbolizes his commitment to the well-being of his people and his determination to uphold Nuada's kingship despite the physical impediment. Dian Cecht's contribution extends beyond the mere mending of flesh; it signifies his devotion to preserving the unity and strength of the Tuatha Dé Danann community.

Nuada's Silver Arm

Nuada, the king with the silver arm, is an epitome of strength in the face of adversity and a symbol of the divine right to rule. His silver arm stands not only as a testament to the advanced magical craftsmanship of the Tuatha Dé Danann, but also as a reminder of the sacrifices made in pursuit of leadership. Nuada's silver arm is emblematic of his resilience and the collective resilience of the Tuatha Dé Danann, reflecting their ability to overcome seemingly insurmountable challenges.

The tale of Nuada's silver arm is intricately woven into the fabric of the Battle of Magh Tuireadh. The loss of his arm in the battle underscores the harsh realities of conflict and the sacrifices made for the greater good. Dian Cecht's creation of the silver arm speaks to the divine

interconnections within the pantheon, where each member contributes their unique talents to sustain the community as a whole.
Moreover, Nuada's silver arm represents a metaphorical bridge between the divine and mortal realms. It signifies the divine influence and protection that the Tuatha Dé Danann offer to the mortal world, a concept deeply embedded in Irish mythology. Nuada's leadership, despite the physical transformation brought about by the silver arm, signifies his enduring strength and his capacity to rule with wisdom and compassion.

The Divine Pantheon of the Tuatha Dé Danann is replete with multifaceted deities, each contributing to the intricate tapestry of Irish mythology. Dian Cecht's healing skills and Nuada's silver arm stand as indelible symbols, embodying themes of healing, resilience, sacrifice, and leadership. Their narratives not only inspire awe but also offer insights into the values and ideals cherished by the Ancient Celts, echoing through the annals of time as a testament to the enduring power of myth and legend.

His role in the pantheon's well-being and health
In the intricate tapestry of the Tuatha Dé Danann, the divine pantheon of Irish mythology, each god and goddess contributes uniquely to the harmony and vitality of their realm. Among these revered figures, Dian Cecht emerges as a pivotal deity, holding a vital role in the well-being and health of both his fellow Tuatha Dé Danann and the broader mythological landscape. Through his mastery of healing arts, his intricate relationship with Nuada, and his symbolic significance, Dian Cecht shapes the very essence of the pantheon's vitality. Dian Cecht's reputation as the preeminent healer among the Tuatha Dé Danann is a cornerstone of his significance. His command over the intricate realm of healing arts sets him apart as a deity capable of mending even the most grievous wounds and ailments. His talents encompass not only physical healing but also the restoration of spiritual and emotional well-being. The herbs and incantations he wields are woven into the fabric of his character, illustrating his profound connection with the forces of rejuvenation and recovery.

Symbolic Significance

Dian Cecht's significance extends beyond his practical contributions to the pantheon. He embodies the essential balance required for the well-being of any divine realm. As a healer, he mends not only the corporeal wounds, but also the underlying rifts and conflicts that threaten the harmony of the Tuatha Dé Danann. His presence serves as a reminder that healing goes beyond the mending of the body; it encompasses the healing of relationships, divisions, and the restoration of unity. Dian Cecht's role resonates with broader themes woven throughout Irish mythology. His dedication to healing mirrors the broader theme of restoration and renewal that underscores many myths. The act of healing—whether through the mending of wounds or the restoration of a sense of purpose—embodies the cyclical nature of life, death, and rebirth. This thematic resonance positions Dian Cecht as a figure who not only tends to the health of the pantheon but also embodies the very essence of its enduring vitality.

Legacy and Lessons

Dian Cecht's legacy endures as a testament to the importance of healing, unity, and the commitment to the well-being of a community. His character serves as a source of inspiration, inviting reflection on the healing potential that exists within each individual and the collective. His relationship with Nuada, embodied in the silver arm, encapsulates the profound impact of collaboration and sacrifice in preserving the pantheon's equilibrium.

In the divine pantheon of the Tuatha Dé Danann, Dian Cecht emerges as a guardian of well-being and health, a healer whose expertise extends beyond the physical realm. His mastery of healing arts, his involvement in the creation of Nuada's silver arm, and the symbolic significance he embodies collectively illustrate his profound role in maintaining the pantheon's vitality. Through his character, one is reminded of the power of healing, unity, and the interconnectedness that binds the divine fabric of Irish mythology together.

Danu: Mother Goddess and Ancestral Source

Danu's Motherly Role in the Tuatha Dé Danann

Danu emerges as a central force, embodying the essence of motherhood, fertility, and nurturing care. Danu, the mother goddess of the Tuatha Dé Danann, stands as a symbol of fertility, creation, and abundance. Revered as the matriarchal force that birthed the divine race, her name itself bears the echoes of nurturing and maternal care. The term "Danu" is linguistically connected to words representing water, rivers, and life-giving sources, highlighting her role as the generative force that sustains life. Central to Danu's portrayal is her role as a mother figure. Her influence is felt not only in the natural world's fertility, but also in the prosperity and abundance experienced by the Tuatha Dé Danann. She is celebrated as the source of life, responsible for the proliferation of beings that constitute the pantheon. This aspect of her character evokes the image of a nurturing deity, ensuring the continuity and vitality of her divine progeny.

Triadic Nature: Maiden, Mother, Crone

Danu's significance deepens with her association with the triadic nature of the goddess, encompassing the aspects of maiden, mother, and crone. As a maiden, she embodies the youthful potential and untamed energy of creation. As a mother, she personifies fertility, care, and the nurturing love that sustains growth. The crone aspect symbolizes wisdom, experience, and the cyclical nature of existence. This trinity encapsulates the entirety of the female life journey and echoes the seasons of life and nature. The festival of Imbolc, dedicated to the goddess Brigid, offers a vivid example of how Danu's motherly essence permeates the Tuatha Dé Danann's traditions. Brigid, associated with healing, poetry, and fertility, embodies the nurturing aspects of Danu's character. Imbolc, marking the arrival of spring and the renewal of life, is a testament to Danu's role in the cycle of seasons and the perpetual rejuvenation of the earth.

Danu's motherly role extends beyond mythology into the cultural fabric of Ireland. Her presence underscores the reverence for nature and the interconnectedness between human life and the natural world. Her image resonates with the deep-rooted appreciation for the land's bounty, the cycle of growth and harvest, and the perpetual renewal that characterizes life's journey.

In the tapestry of the Tuatha Dé Danann, Danu's motherly role weaves a thread of nurturing care, fertility, and abundance. As the mother goddess, she stands as a divine embodiment of the creative force that shapes existence, sustains life, and ensures the continuation of the pantheon's legacy. Danu's presence transcends the realms of mythology, inspiring a profound connection with the cycles of nature and the eternal dance of creation and renewal.

Danu's Symbolic Connection to the Land and Fertility
The Mother Goddess and Matriarch Danu, often referred to as the mother goddess of the Tuatha Dé Danann, is a figure of immense significance within Celtic mythology. She is considered not only the ancestor of the Tuatha Dé Danann, but also the embodiment of the land itself. Her name, derived from the Proto-Celtic word for "river," evokes the idea of flowing waters that nourish and sustain the earth. As a mother figure, Danu is associated with fertility, growth, and the life-giving forces that underpin the natural world. Danu's symbolism is closely intertwined with fertility and abundance, themes that are central to both agricultural societies and the understanding of the divine. She represents the bountiful aspect of the earth, providing sustenance for plants, animals, and humans alike. The image of Danu as a mother nurturing the land reflects the cyclical rhythms of nature, where the seasons bring forth life, growth, harvest, and renewal.

Danu and the Land
Sacred Relationship The connection between Danu and the land is a reciprocal one, representing a sacred relationship between the divine and the material world. The earth itself is considered a manifestation of Danu's presence, making the very act of cultivating the land a form of devotion to her. This symbiotic relationship underscores the importance

of stewardship and the respectful use of natural resources—an ethos that carries resonance even in contemporary times.

One of the most prominent celebrations associated with Danu is the festival of Imbolc. Occurring around the beginning of February, Imbolc marks the first stirrings of spring and is dedicated to Brigid, the triple goddess closely associated with Danu. This festival is a testament to Danu's role as the source of life and growth, as the land begins to awaken from its winter slumber. The symbolic connection between Danu and the land remains a potent theme in modern Irish culture. The reverence for the earth's fertility and the cyclical nature of life has been preserved through the generations, underscoring the enduring impact of mythological narratives. Even as societies have evolved, the reverence for the land and its life-giving qualities continues to be a guiding principle, reflecting the wisdom embedded within the stories of Danu and the Tuatha Dé Danann.

Danu's Enduring Legacy

The symbolism of Danu's connection to the land and fertility encapsulates the essence of the divine pantheon of the Tuatha Dé Danann. Her role as the mother goddess and the embodiment of the earth's life-giving forces transcends time, resonating with ancient agricultural practices, spiritual beliefs, and the cultural identity of the Irish people. Through her enduring legacy, Danu invites us to recognize the profound interconnectedness between humanity, nature, and the divine—a lesson that remains as relevant today as it was in the myths of old.

Bres: Mixed Ancestry and Kingship

Bres's Dual Heritage and Struggles as a King

Bres stands as a significant character whose dual heritage and struggles as a king provide profound insights into the complexities of leadership, identity, and the ever-evolving dynamics within the divine pantheon.

Bres's unique lineage is emblematic of the interconnectedness of various mythological realms. He is the product of a union between Eriu, a Tuatha Dé Danann goddess representing Ireland itself, and Elatha, a Fomorian king. This dual heritage, with one foot in the Tuatha Dé Danann world and the other in the Fomorian domain, underscores Bres's role as a bridge between two conflicting forces.

Bres's mixed heritage places him in an intricate web of expectations and aspirations. His Fomorian heritage marks him as an outsider within the Tuatha Dé Danann pantheon, while his divine lineage entitles him to a claim for leadership. This internal struggle for acceptance, coupled with his desire to fulfill the role of a king, encapsulates his poignant journey.

Bres's Ascension to Kingship

Bres's ascent to kingship, despite his mixed parentage, raises questions about the criteria for leadership within the Tuatha Dé Danann. Upon Nuada's injury in the Battle of Magh Tuireadh, Bres assumes the role of king. His reign, however, is fraught with challenges as his rule embodies an uneasy compromise between the Tuatha Dé Danann and the Fomorians, leading to tensions within his court. Bres's rule is marked by discord, as he struggles to balance the conflicting interests of his Fomorian lineage and his responsibilities as a Tuatha Dé Danann king. His attempts to impose heavy taxes on his subjects, influenced by Fomorian values, lead to widespread dissatisfaction and unrest. This internal turmoil reflects the broader struggles between the two mythological races and the complexities of coexistence.

The Fall of Bres

Bres's inability to effectively unite the Tuatha Dé Danann under his rule culminates in his eventual downfall. His rule of compromise becomes untenable, and the mantle of leadership falls to Lugh, a god with a more holistic understanding of the Tuatha Dé Danann's identity and values. Bres's dethronement signifies a return to a leadership model more closely aligned with the pantheon's inherent ideals and aspirations. Bres's narrative is not merely a tale of a fallen king; it is a profound exploration of identity, leadership, and the clash of cultures. His struggles as a leader torn between conflicting allegiances serve as a cautionary tale about the pitfalls of compromising core values for expedient alliances. Bres's journey teaches that true leadership arises from an authentic understanding of one's heritage and the ability to harmonize it with the greater good of the community.

Bres's dual heritage and struggles as a king within the divine pantheon of the Tuatha Dé Danann are a microcosm of the broader tensions that define mythology itself. His complex lineage and attempts to navigate the treacherous waters of leadership underscore the perpetual struggle to find balance between divergent forces. Bres's story speaks to the eternal human quest for self-discovery, the complexities of identity, and the intricate nature of leadership in the face of adversity.

Bres's Interactions with the Fomorians and the Tuatha Dé Danann

The realm of Irish mythology is replete with a diverse cast of gods and goddesses, each contributing unique qualities and narratives to the overarching tapestry of Celtic lore. Among these figures, Bres, a character of complex origins and intricate connections, holds a significant place within the divine pantheon. His interactions with both the Fomorians and the Tuatha Dé Danann serve as a captivating tale that underscores themes of diplomacy, leadership, and the intricate relationships between opposing forces. Bres's lineage is emblematic of the intricate interplay between divine beings in Irish mythology. His father, Elatha of the Fomorians, and his mother, Eriu of the Tuatha Dé Danann, represent the intricate connections that often transcend boundaries between the divine races. Bres's mixed parentage positions him as a bridge between two warring factions, with the potential to either unite or further divide them.

The Fomorians and the Tuatha Dé Danann stand as opposing forces in Irish mythology, embodying a dichotomy between chaos and order. Bres, with his lineage linking both factions, is placed at the center of this cosmic struggle. His interactions with each group illuminate the complex dynamics at play.

Bres Among the Fomorians

Upon discovering his father's identity, Bres gains entry into the world of the Fomorians. However, his experience among them is marked by a sense of estrangement due to his Tuatha Dé Danann heritage. Despite this, Bres's longing for acceptance drives him to seek out alliances that could benefit both his father's people and his own aspirations.Bres's interactions with the Fomorians and the Tuatha Dé Danann underscore themes of identity, diplomacy, and the tension between personal aspirations and societal obligations. His journey highlights the challenges faced by those who straddle opposing factions, negotiating allegiances in pursuit of unity.

Bres's presence in the divine pantheon of Irish mythology serves as a bridge between warring factions, embodying the intricate relationships and moral dilemmas that define the cosmos of Celtic lore. His story resonates with the complexities of leadership, diplomacy, and the pursuit of unity in a world marked by cosmic conflict. Bres's interactions with the Fomorians and the Tuatha Dé Danann illuminate the broader themes of identity, compromise, and the multifaceted nature of divinity within the rich tapestry of Irish mythological narratives.

Midir: Lord of the Underworld and Love

Midir's Connection to the Otherworld and the Land of the Dead

Midir stands as a captivating enigma, whose association with the Otherworld and the land of the dead adds depth and complexity to the Tuatha Dé Danann pantheon.

Midir, often depicted as a god of immense beauty and wisdom, occupies a distinctive place within the Tuatha Dé Danann. He is renowned for his enigmatic nature and is celebrated as a deity whose presence bridges the gap between the Otherworld and the realm of the living. His stories often revolve around love, loss, and the ethereal realm beyond mortal comprehension.

One of Midir's most defining characteristics is his intimate connection to the Otherworld, a realm of sublime beauty and mystique that lies beyond the confines of the human world. It is within this realm that the Tuatha Dé Danann are said to reside, and Midir's association with it cements his status as a guardian of its secrets and mysteries. Through his interactions and escapades, Midir provides a glimpse into this realm, blurring the lines between the mundane and the supernatural.

Midir and the Land of the Dead Midir's significance also extends to the land of the dead, a realm that holds a unique place in various cultures' mythologies. He is often linked to the concept of death and rebirth, with his narratives intertwining with themes of mortality and transcendence. In some accounts, Midir is portrayed as a guide who assists souls in their journey from the mortal realm to the afterlife, exemplifying his dual role as both a guardian and a bridge between worlds.

Midir's tale is intrinsically tied to themes of love, loss, and unwavering persistence. His pursuit of the fairy maiden Étaín, across lifetimes and challenges, showcases his dedication and determination. This narrative further emphasizes his connection to the Otherworld, as well as his position as a deity who navigates the complex interplay of destiny and human emotions. Midir's role as a mediator between the Otherworld and the realm of the living carries profound cultural and symbolic implications. He embodies the idea that the boundaries between life and death, reality and enchantment, are not as rigid as they seem. His stories reflect a belief in the interconnectedness of existence and the possibility of transcending the limitations of mortality.

Legacy and Contemporary Relevance
Midir's legacy extends beyond the pages of ancient texts, influencing literature, art, and cultural expression to this day. His character continues to inspire creators who seek to explore the intricate relationship between humans and the unseen forces that shape their world. Midir's portrayal serves as a reminder of the enduring power of mythology to inspire contemplation and creativity.

Midir's connection to the Otherworld and the land of the dead enriches the Divine Pantheon of the Tuatha Dé Danann with layers of mysticism, depth, and significance. His role as a guardian, guide, and enigmatic figure blurs the lines between worlds, inviting us to contemplate the profound interplay between life, death, and the realms beyond. Midir's presence serves as a timeless reminder that mythology transcends time, offering us glimpses into the mysteries that continue to captivate our imagination.

Midir's Tragic Love Story with Étaín
In the intricate tapestry of Irish mythology, the divine pantheon of the Tuatha Dé Danann is replete with tales of love, heroism, and tragedy. Among these captivating stories, the tragic love affair between Midir and Étaín stands as a poignant and enduring example of the complexities of love, fate, and the Otherworldly realm. The Mysterious Noble Midir, a prominent figure within the Tuatha Dé Danann, is often depicted as a noble and mysterious god associated with the Otherworld. His name evokes a sense of enigma, reflecting the veil that separates his realm from the mortal world. Midir is revered for his remarkable appearance and enchanting demeanor, which earned him a place among the pantheon's most intriguing members. Étaín, on the other hand, is a beautiful and radiant mortal woman who inadvertently finds herself entangled in the Otherworldly affairs of the divine. Her existence bridges the gap between the human realm and the ethereal

domain of the Tuatha Dé Danann, setting the stage for a love story that transcends the boundaries of reality.

The Fateful Meeting and Enchantment
The tale begins with Midir's enchantment upon seeing Étaín. Captivated by her beauty, he is compelled to make her a part of his world. However, Étaín is already bound by mortal ties, having been married to a human nobleman named Eochaid Airem. Despite Midir's supernatural charm, Étaín initially resists his advances, remaining steadfast in her loyalty to her husband. Midir's love for Étaín faces numerous obstacles, chief among them being Étaín's marital commitment. The struggle between mortal life and the allure of the Otherworld unfolds in a series of events that sees Midir employing his magical abilities to navigate the challenges. In his pursuit of happiness with Étaín, Midir's actions disrupt the delicate balance between the human and divine realms, leading to unforeseen consequences.

In the midst of their complex relationship, Étaín undergoes a series of transformative experiences. As she encounters obstacles, betrayals, and separations, her identity and physical form are altered. These transformations add layers of tragedy and depth to the narrative, illustrating the fleeting nature of mortal existence and the profound influence of the Otherworld on the lives of humans. The eternal love lost and regained despite Midir's unwavering love and Étaín's deep affection for him, their path is marked by tragic separations and heartache. The narrative highlights the themes of destiny, sacrifice, and the ephemeral nature of human life. Midir's persistent efforts to reunite with Étaín showcase his dedication and the lengths he is willing to go for the sake of their love.

A Tale of Love and Loss
The tale of Midir and Étaín stands as a testament to the power of love that defies the boundaries of time and existence. Their story reflects the inherent conflict between mortality and the Otherworld, showcasing the complexities of human emotions when intertwined with the divine. Through the characters of Midir and Étaín, Irish mythology paints a poignant portrayal of the human experience, replete with joy, sorrow, and the enduring legacy of love that transcends both life and death.

Chapter 3
The Four Treasures of the Tuatha Dé Danann

Unveiling the Magic and Legacy

In the realm where myth and reality intertwine, the Tuatha Dé Danann, a divine race of beings, held dominion over ancient Ireland. Within their mystical grasp rested four treasures of remarkable power—artifacts infused with magic and meaning that resonated with the very heart of Irish culture. As we delve into the stories of these Four Treasures, we uncover not only their historical significance, but also the deep mythology and enduring impact that have woven themselves into the fabric of modern Ireland.

1. The Sword of Nuada: Claíomh Solais

In the heart of Nuada's illustrious reign rested the magnificent Claíomh Solais, the Sword of Light, a weapon whose origins were steeped in the mystical fires of the Otherworld. Its blade, resplendent and radiant, shimmered with an ethereal luminescence that had the extraordinary ability to banish the darkest shadows and ignite a fervor of courage within the hearts of all who gazed upon it. Yet, beyond its sheer practicality in the heat of battle, the Claíomh Solais bore profound symbolism as well. This legendary sword stood as a testament to Nuada's authority and his unwavering commitment to justice. It served as an embodiment of the notion that true leadership was a harmonious blend of raw strength and sagacious wisdom—a potent reminder that authentic power did not solely reside in martial prowess, but also in the profound capacity to kindle the flames of inspiration and illuminate the path of righteousness for all who followed.

Legend whispered that this extraordinary sword had been forged in the crucible of the Otherworld, where the elemental fires themselves had lent their magic to its creation. Its origin story was a tale that intertwined the mortal realm with the mystical, a narrative woven into the very fabric of Nuada's destiny as a leader. The Claíomh Solais was no ordinary weapon; it was a symbol of hope and virtue. Its mere presence at Nuada's side during his reign was a source of reassurance for his people, a beacon of unwavering resolve in the face of adversity, and a symbol of the enduring connection between the mortal world and the realm of the divine.

2. The Spear of Lugh: Gáe Bulg

Lugh, the god renowned for his multifaceted talents, bore aloft the Gáe Bulg, a weapon that transcended mere craftsmanship; it was an emblem of divine artistry and enchantment. Forged with meticulous precision and imbued with the very essence of tempestuous storms, the Gáe Bulg possessed a menace all its own. Its barbed tips, each a symphony of divine intent, were renowned for their ability to puncture even the most impervious of defenses. The origins of this extraordinary spear are veiled in mythic mystique. Wrought for a singular purpose—to guarantee triumph in the fateful Battle of Magh Tuireadh—the Gáe Bulg transcended the realm of ordinary weaponry. Its creation was a testament to the harmonious interplay of skill, strategy, and raw power.

The Gáe Bulg's enchantment whispered secrets of thunderclouds and lightning bolts, channeling the very essence of storms. With a thrust of this celestial weapon, the skies themselves seemed to roar in approval. In the hands of Lugh, it became an extension of his divine prowess, a symbol of his mastery over both the natural and supernatural realms. As Lugh unfurled the Gáe Bulg upon the battlefield, his adversaries could feel the palpable weight of impending doom. Its barbed tips, said to transform into a multitude upon impact, ensured that no armor, no matter how formidable, could withstand its relentless assault. The very act of unleashing the spear was a proclamation of dominance, a declaration that victory was not a mere possibility but an inevitability. The Gáe Bulg, with its thunderous origins and the godly might it personified, stands as a testament to the intersection of myth and reality, where divine craftsmanship met the exigencies of battle, ultimately etching its name into the annals of legend.

3. The Stone of Destiny: Lia Fáil

Perched majestically atop the sacred hill of Tara, the Stone of Destiny, known as Lia Fáil, stands as an ancient sentinel, a timeless witness to the ebb and flow of Irish kings throughout the ages. This enigmatic monolith, its moss-covered steps steeped in history, possesses an aura that transcends mere stone and mortar. Those who ascend these hallowed steps are met with a profound resonance, an elusive vibration that seems to harmonize with the very essence of the land itself. Legend has it that Lia Fáil possesses a unique and mystical quality: the stone is believed to roar in recognition of a true king. This ethereal phenomenon encapsulates the profound connection between sovereignty and leadership in Celtic tradition. It goes beyond a mere ceremonial gesture; it serves as a living embodiment of the sacred bond between ruler and realm. Yet, Lia Fáil is more than a symbol of kingship; it is a manifestation of the profound and symbiotic relationship that exists between the ruler and the land they govern. The stone whispers a timeless tale of unity, reminding all who hear of the profound and shared destiny that binds the people and their leaders. It reflects a deep-rooted belief that genuine leadership is not merely an assertion of dominance, but a sacred commitment to stewardship and guardianship. Lia Fáil serves as a steadfast reminder that the welfare of the land and the well-being of its inhabitants are intricately intertwined with the actions and intentions of those who hold the mantle of power.

Today, despite the passage of countless centuries, the Stone of Destiny, Lia Fáil, continues to stand in all its mystic glory upon the venerable Hill of Tara, nestled in the heart of County Meath. This historic and enduring symbol of Irish kingship, draped in the weight of its age-old legacy, remains a poignant reminder of the enduring values of leadership, unity, and the profound connection between a people and their land. It is here, amidst the whispers of history and the echoes of ancient roars, that the story of Lia Fáil continues to unfold.

4. The Cauldron of the Dagda: Coire Ansic

In the hands of the Dagda, the mighty Cauldron of Abundance, Coire Ansic, was a vessel of sustenance and healing. The cauldron possessed the remarkable ability to provide an unending feast, nurturing not only bodies but also spirits. This enchanting cauldron underscored the themes of generosity, community, and the idea that sharing nourishment was an act of magic in itself. Coire Ansic served as a metaphor for the nurturing aspect of leadership—the responsibility to provide for and uplift the community. Just as the cauldron replenished those who partook, leaders were tasked with ensuring the well-being of their people, nurturing their potential and fostering an environment of prosperity.

The Impact on Modern Irish Culture
The legacy of the Four Treasures of the Tuatha Dé Danann is not confined to the annals of history; it reverberates through the corridors of modern Irish culture, infusing it with ancient wisdom and symbolism. In literature and art, these treasures serve as metaphors for enduring values. The Claíomh Solais becomes a beacon for leaders who seek to inspire and guide with both strength and wisdom. The Gáe Bulg resonates with individuals who understand that the mastery of one's craft is a path to success. The Stone of Destiny finds echoes in the hearts of those who navigate leadership roles with integrity and compassion. The Cauldron of Abundance speaks to the importance of communal well-being and nurturing the bonds that unite a society.

Echoes of Ancient Magic
As we gently draw the curtain on the tales of the Four Treasures, it becomes abundantly clear that these magnificent artifacts are far from mere relics of a bygone era; they are, in every sense, living symbols that persist in their ability to inspire, guide, and deeply connect the Irish people. These stories, like whispers from the distant past, refuse to fade, serving as an unwavering testament to the timeless wisdom that transcends the boundaries of generations. The Four Treasures of the Tuatha Dé Danann stand resolute, unbroken bridges, capable of forging a profound link between the past and the present. They are the threads that intricately weave a narrative that finds its way into the very core of Irish culture. This culture, with its mythic underpinnings, not only endures but thrives in the face of modernity's intricate challenges, doing so with an inherent grace and purpose. Just as the Claíomh Solais, with its radiant glow, illuminates the path of leadership, the Gáe Bulg, with its fateful sting, pierces through the toughest of challenges. The Lia Fáil, the stone of destiny, resounds with echoes of unity between its people and their sacred land. Lastly, the Coire Ansic, the cauldron of plenty, nurtures the unbreakable bonds of community. These Four Treasures, each in its own unique way, stand as enduring testaments to the unyielding magic that flows ceaselessly through the veins of Irish heritage, a wellspring of strength, inspiration, and timeless connection.

Chapter 4
Kingship and Leadership

The importance of kingship among the Tuatha Dé Danann

In the realm of Irish mythology, the Tuatha Dé Danann stand as a remarkable group of divine beings whose intricate society is characterized by profound complexities, each element holding deep symbolic significance. Among these elements, the concept of kingship and leadership shines as a beacon of authority, responsibility, and societal structure. The importance of kingship among the Tuatha Dé Danann is not merely a narrative thread, but rather a reflection of their cultural values, the order they sought to establish, and the lessons they imparted through their stories.

1. *Divine Authority and Representation:* Kingship among the Tuatha Dé Danann was not simply a mortal role; it was a divine mandate that transcended the realm of humans. The king was chosen not solely for his martial prowess, but also for his wisdom, fairness, and connections to the divine. The king was perceived as a representative of the gods, a figure entrusted with the responsibility of guiding his people in harmony with the cosmic order. This idea reinforced the link between the divine and mortal worlds, emphasizing the interconnectedness of all existence
2. *The Symbolism of Wholeness:* Nuada, the king with the silver arm, epitomizes the symbolic significance of kingship within the Tuatha Dé Danann society. His loss of a hand and the subsequent replacement with a silver arm underscored the concept of the king as the embodiment of the entire community. Just as his arm was made whole through ingenuity and collaboration, so too was the kingdom bound together under his rule. This symbolism of wholeness and restoration was a cornerstone of kingship, reminding the Tuatha Dé Danann of the unity that underpins a successful realm.
3. *Leadership in Times of Crisis:* The narratives surrounding kingship often revolve around challenges and crises that test the king's mettle and character. The Battle of Magh Tuireadh serves as a crucible wherein Nuada's leadership is put to the ultimate test. His resilience, courage,

and strategic acumen during this battle elevate him as a symbol of steadfast leadership in the face of adversity. This exemplifies the Tuatha Dé Danann's belief in the pivotal role of the king as a guiding light even in the darkest of times.

4. *Transition and the Evolution of Leadership:* The transition from Nuada to Lugh as king exemplifies the fluidity and adaptability of the Tuatha Dé Danann's leadership structure. Lugh, a multi-skilled god and a heroic figure, represents a new era of leadership marked by versatility, innovation, and a broader range of talents. This transition highlights the community's willingness to embrace change and harness the strengths of different individuals for the greater good.

5. *Lessons for Mortals:* The concept of kingship among the Tuatha Dé Danann offers valuable lessons for mortals. It underscores the importance of just and benevolent leadership, where the welfare of the people takes precedence. Moreover, it reminds mortals of the interconnectedness of all aspects of life, urging them to recognize the divine in the mundane and to uphold integrity and unity in their own societies.

The importance of kingship among the Tuatha Dé Danann extends beyond the realm of myth and storytelling. It is a reflection of their cultural ethos, a blueprint for societal harmony, and a reminder of the profound responsibilities that come with leadership. Through the lens of kingship, the Tuatha Dé Danann impart timeless wisdom about the essence of authority, the virtues of leadership, and the role of the divine in shaping the course of history.

The concept of divine leadership and its responsibilities

In Irish mythology, the concept of kingship and leadership holds a significant place, especially within the realm of the Tuatha Dé Danann. These divine beings, often referred to as gods, embody not only the extraordinary but also the complexities of leadership that extend beyond mortal boundaries. The theme of kingship is interwoven with the ideals of responsibility, sacrifice, and the intricate balance between power and duty. The notion of kingship in Celtic mythology is deeply rooted in the divine. Kings were not just political leaders but spiritual figures, bridging the mortal and Otherworldly realms. Among the Tuatha Dé Danann, the selection of a king was not solely based on lineage but on a combination of wisdom, strength, and divine favor. The divine lineage of these gods emphasized their unique qualities, setting them apart from mortals and underscoring their suitability for leadership.

Divine Responsibilities

The role of a divine king extended far beyond mundane governance. It encompassed the well-being of the land, the prosperity of the people, and the maintenance of cosmic order. The Tuatha Dé Danann kings were charged with safeguarding the Otherworld and Earth, fostering the growth of crops, ensuring harmony in relationships, and upholding the cultural and spiritual fabric of their society. This multifaceted responsibility went beyond traditional governance and embraced a sacred duty to maintain balance in all aspects of existence. Leadership among the Tuatha Dé Danann was not without its challenges. Rivalries with other divine groups, such as the Fomorians, demanded careful diplomacy and strategy. The relationships forged between leaders and other deities, as well as with humans, showcased the complex interplay between power dynamics, alliances, and the pursuit of collective goals. The transition of kingship, from Nuada to Lugh in the aftermath of the Battle of Magh Tuireadh, highlighted the fluid nature of leadership. Lugh's ascension demonstrated the necessity of adaptability and the embodiment of diverse qualities in leaders. This transition also spoke to the cyclic nature of leadership, where the old gives way to the new while maintaining continuity.

Lessons for Mortals

The concept of divine kingship within the Tuatha Dé Danann mythology offers profound lessons for mortal leaders and society at large. It emphasizes the importance of visionary thinking, a deep understanding of the interconnectedness of all things, and the necessity of making difficult decisions for the betterment of the community. Moreover, it highlights the idea that true leadership is an embodiment of service, sacrifice, and the ability to maintain harmony amidst adversity. The concept of kingship and leadership among the Tuatha Dé Danann serves as a captivating exploration of the intricate relationship between the divine and the mortal. It underscores that leadership is not solely about wielding power, but about assuming the profound responsibilities that come with it. The stories of these divine kings provide a timeless and universal insight into the ideals and challenges of leadership that continue to resonate across cultures and epochs.

Transition from Nuada to Lugh: Implications and lessons
The transition of leadership within the realm of the Tuatha Dé Danann, from King Nuada to King Lugh, serves as a profound and instructive narrative, offering insights into the qualities of a ruler, power dynamics, and the balance between tradition and innovation. Nuada, the King with the Silver Arm Nuada Airgetlám's initial reign as the monarch of the Tuatha Dé Danann was characterized by wisdom, astute leadership, and a divine lineage that justified his rule. Under his guidance, the people prospered, and he adeptly steered them through numerous challenges. However, a significant setback occurred when he lost his arm during a battle against the Fir Bolg, leading to a temporary dethronement. It was the skilled healer, Dian Cecht, who ingeniously crafted a silver arm for Nuada, thus enabling his return to the throne.

The symbolism of Nuada's silver arm extended beyond mere physical restoration. It embodied his unwavering determination to fulfill his kingly duties despite formidable obstacles. Nuada's ability to adapt and embrace innovation, as evidenced by the acceptance of his prosthetic arm, serves as a poignant lesson in resilience and the importance of adaptive leadership. Lugh, the Heroic, Multifaceted Leader The ascension of Lugh Lámhfhada to the throne marked a pivotal juncture in the Tuatha Dé Danann's history. Lugh's reputation as a god of multifaceted talents, excelling in combat, magic, and artistry, heralded a new era of leadership. His arrival was seen as a beacon of hope, and his ability to unite these diverse talents proved invaluable. Lugh's coronation coincided with his heroic role in the Battle of Magh Tuireadh, a momentous victory against the Fomorians, which showcased his strategic brilliance.

The transition from Nuada to Lugh underscores the importance of recognizing and appreciating a leader's multifaceted talents. Lugh's capacity to bridge various domains highlighted the value of versatility and adaptability, attributes that allowed him to excel in the face of ever-changing circumstances. His triumphs illuminate the significance of strategic thinking and innovation within leadership.

Implications and Lessons The transition from Nuada to Lugh resonates beyond mythology, offering profound implications and enduring lessons:

1. *Adaptive Leadership:* Nuada's resilience and adaptability in the face of adversity underscore the necessity of adaptive leadership. His ability to lead effectively despite physical limitations teaches us the importance of flexibility and creative problem-solving.
2. *Diverse Skillsets:* Lugh's diverse skill set emphasizes the value of a leader who possesses a wide range of talents. His ability to excel in multiple domains demonstrates that a leader's proficiency need not be confined to a single area, but can encompass a spectrum of skills.
3. *Innovation and Tradition:* The transition from Nuada to Lugh highlights the interplay between tradition and innovation. While Nuada's acceptance of the silver arm allowed him to uphold tradition, Lugh's diverse talents showcased the importance of embracing new approaches while respecting existing customs.
4. *Strategic Brilliance:* Lugh's strategic brilliance in the Battle of Magh Tuireadh reinforces the significance of strategic thinking in leadership. His ability to analyze situations, devise effective plans, and rally his forces reflects the potency of foresight and planning.

The transition from Nuada to Lugh within the realm of the Tuatha Dé Danann epitomizes leadership as a dynamic interplay of qualities that evolve with time, experience, and the needs of the people. It serves as a timeless reminder that leadership is not a static concept, but a fluid, ever-evolving force that shapes the destinies of both mortal and immortal realms alike.

Chapter 5
Devine Battles for Ireland and the Exodus to the Otherworld

The Fir Bolg: The Forgotten Inhabitants of Irish Mythology
In the rich tapestry of Irish mythology, the Fir Bolg emerge as a compelling but often overshadowed group of beings who once held sway over the mystical land of Ireland. These enigmatic figures, while not as well-known as the Tuatha Dé Danann or the Fomorians, occupy a significant place in the lore of ancient Ireland.

Origins and Etymology
The origins of the Fir Bolg are shrouded in mystery, much like many mythological beings. The name "Fir Bolg" is believed to have roots in Old Irish, with "Fir" meaning "men" and "Bolg" being a subject of interpretation. Some scholars suggest that "Bolg" might be related to the Old Irish word "bolg," meaning "belly" or "bag," while others propose connections to the word "bolc" or "bolg," which could imply "sack" or "baggage." These interpretations hint at associations with physical characteristics or perhaps even nomadic origins. The arrival of the Fir Bolg in Ireland is a pivotal moment in Irish mythology. Legend has it that they came to Ireland from distant lands, possibly fleeing from oppression or seeking new territories. Upon their arrival, they encountered the Tuatha Dé Danann. This encounter set the stage for a series of confrontations and alliances, marking the Fir Bolg's place in Irish myth.

The First Battle of Magh Tuireadh: Fir Bolg vs. Tuatha Dé Danann
The First Battle of Magh Tuireadh, a conflict between the Fir Bolg and the Tuatha Dé Danann, serves as a pivotal event in the mythology. In this battle, the Fir Bolg, led by their king Eochaid mac Eirc, confronted the Tuatha Dé Danann, whose leader at the time was King Nuada.
The outcome of the battle was marked by shifting fortunes. King Nuada lost his arm in combat, symbolically losing his authority as the ruler.

However, the Fir Bolg were not without their own losses. The battle ended inconclusively, setting the stage for further conflicts.

The Second Battle of Magh Tuireadh, also known as Cath Maighe Tuireadh or the Battle of Moytura, is a significant event in Irish mythology. It is one of the key battles that shaped the early history of Ireland and is a central episode in the legendary tales of the Tuatha Dé Danann and the Fir Bolg. This battle is recorded in several ancient Irish texts, including the Lebor Gabála Érenn (The Book of Invasions) and the Cath Maige Tuired (The Second Battle of Magh Tuireadh). The Second Battle of Magh Tuireadh was fought because the Fir Bolg's leadership had become oppressive and tyrannical. Bres, a half-Fomorian king, ruled the Tuatha Dé Danann at this time, and his harsh reign led to discontent among his people. The Tuatha Dé Danann sought to overthrow Bres and regain control of Ireland. To do so, they needed the help of Lugh Lamfada, a heroic figure known for his many talents, including warrior skills and wisdom. Lugh challenged Bres to single combat and defeated him, ultimately taking control of the Tuatha Dé Danann. With Lugh as their leader, the Tuatha Dé Danann prepared for the Second Battle of Magh Tuireadh. They assembled their forces, which included warriors, druids, and magical beings, and faced the Fir Bolg in a fierce and epic battle.

In the Second Battle of Magh Tuireadh, the Tuatha Dé Danann emerged victorious once again. The Fir Bolg were defeated, and their leader, Eochaid mac Eirc, was killed. The battle marked the final victory of the Tuatha Dé Danann, who subsequently became the dominant supernatural race in Ireland.

Fate of the Fir Bolg

After their defeat, the Fir Bolg's presence in Ireland dwindled. Some were said to have retreated to the remote islands and regions of the country. Others integrated into the society of the Tuatha Dé Danann and took on various roles, while some Fir Bolg were said to have joined the ranks of the Tuatha Dé Danann as craftsmen and artisans. In essence, they became a subjugated people, and their distinct identity gradually faded away. The Second Battle of Magh Tuireadh and the fate of the Fir Bolg are central elements in the complex tapestry of Irish mythology. These legends reflect the cyclical nature of power struggles and the shifting fortunes of the mythological races that inhabited ancient Ireland. While they may be rooted in mythology, these tales hold cultural and historical significance and continue to be treasured in Irish folklore and literature.

The Fir Bolg's legacy in Irish mythology serves as a reflection of the ebb and flow of power, migration, and the encounters that have shaped the island's history. Their presence in the lore of Ireland underscores the complexity of the mythic landscape, where various races and beings coexist, clash, and form alliances. Symbolically, the Fir Bolg represent the idea of migration and the struggles of a displaced people seeking a new home. Their encounters with the Tuatha Dé Danann reflect themes of power dynamics, conflict, and the perennial question of who shall rule over the land. The Fir Bolg, while often overshadowed by other mythological beings, occupy a distinctive place in the intricate tapestry of Irish mythology. Their story is one of migration, conflict, and the enduring impact of encounters between diverse groups within the mythic landscape of Ireland. In their role as protagonists in the First Battle of Magh Tuireadh and their subsequent encounters with the Tuatha Dé Danann, the Fir Bolg's presence is a reminder that the mythology of Ireland is replete with layers, complexities, and tales waiting to be explored and celebrated.

The Fomorians: Enigmatic Forces of Chaos in Irish Mythology
In the realm of Irish mythology, the Fomorians stand as enigmatic and formidable beings, often cast in the role of antagonists. These mysterious entities, while less well-known than the Tuatha Dé Danann, are pivotal to the mythic tapestry of ancient Ireland. To comprehend the depth of their history, significance, and the intricate nature of their existence, one must embark on a journey through the annals of mythology and history to explore the rich details of the Fomorians. The historical origins of the Fomorians are shrouded in the mists of time, as is typical of mythological beings. The name "Fomorian" is believed to be derived from the Old Irish word "fomoire," which intriguingly translates to "underworld dwellers" or "demons of the deep sea." This etymology suggests a profound connection with the sea and the unknown depths—an association that captures the awe and fear inspired by the maritime world in ancient societies.

Within the complex and multifaceted narratives of Irish mythology, the Fomorians emerge as a distinct race of beings, separate from the Tuatha Dé Danann. They are described as monstrous entities, possessing grotesque features such as multiple eyes, limbs, and deformities. Some Fomorians were even said to be giants, their formidable stature reflecting their imposing presence.

Throughout Irish mythology, the Fomorians frequently play the role of antagonists. Their conflicts with the Tuatha Dé Danann, who represent civilization, knowledge, and divine attributes, form the crux of many myths. The most notable of these confrontations is the Battle of Magh Tuireadh, a pivotal event that shapes the Fomorians' legacy.

The Connection to Chaos and Nature

Interpretations of the Fomorians often revolve around the themes of chaos and the untamed forces of nature. They are sometimes seen as embodiments of the primal and uncontrollable aspects of the natural world. In contrast to the Tuatha Dé Danann, who represent order and civilization, the Fomorians stand as a reminder of the chaotic and unpredictable elements of existence. This duality reflects a universal theme in mythology—the eternal struggle between order and chaos, civilization and wilderness. In the mythological landscape, the Fomorians represent the wild, untamed aspects of the world that humanity must contend with.

The Fomorians are perhaps most renowned for their role in epic battles against the Tuatha Dé Danann. The Battle of Magh Tuireadh, mentioned earlier, is the most significant of these confrontations. In this pivotal clash, the Fomorians, led by their fearsome king Balor, sought to maintain their dominance over Ireland. The Tuatha Dé Danann, under the leadership of Nuada and later Lugh, contested their rule.

Central to this battle was Balor's malevolent eye, capable of annihilating with a single glance. Lugh, armed with exceptional skills and intellect, engaged Balor in a dramatic confrontation and vanquished the Fomorian king.

Legacy and Symbolism

The legacy of the Fomorians in Irish mythology is one of complexity and nuance. While often cast as adversaries, they symbolize the profound and intricate dance of life's dualities—order and chaos, civilization and wilderness, known and unknown. They serve as a reminder that the natural world contains both beauty and danger, both the familiar and the mysterious. In the broader context of Irish culture and identity, the Fomorians play a role in shaping the mythic landscape. They embody the challenges and adversities faced by the Tuatha Dé Danann, serving as a means to underscore the strength and resilience of the divine race in their quest for supremacy.

The Fomorians, while less celebrated than other mythological beings, are integral to the rich tapestry of Irish mythology. They represent the wild, chaotic, and untamed forces that coexist with civilization and order. Their stories serve as a reminder of the intricate interplay between opposing forces in the natural world and the enduring power of myth to capture the complexity of human experience. In their role as antagonists to the Tuatha Dé Danann, the Fomorians remind us that the narratives of mythology are not mere tales of good versus evil but reflections of the intricate dance of life's dualities.

The Battle of Magh Tuireadh: Tuatha Dé Danann vs Fomorians
In the annals of Irish mythology, few conflicts are as epic and consequential as the Battle of Magh Tuireadh. This monumental clash, pitting the godlike Tuatha Dé Danann against the formidable Fomorians, represents a pivotal moment in the ancient lore of Ireland. The origins of the Battle of Magh Tuireadh are deeply rooted in the mythic landscape of ancient Ireland. The Tuatha Dé Danann had descended from the heavens to establish their dominion over the island. Their arrival marked a shift in the balance of power, challenging the preexisting rule of the Fomorians. The Fomorians, often depicted as monstrous and otherworldly beings, embodied the chaotic and untamed forces of nature. Led by their imposing king, Balor, who possessed a destructive eye that could slay with a single glance, they sought to maintain their grip on Ireland. This discord set the stage for the Battle of Magh Tuireadh, a clash of gods and titans with the fate of the land hanging in the balance.

The Second Battle of Magh Tuireadh

The Second Battle of Magh Tuireadh or The Northern Magh Tuireadh, often referred to as the main event, was a climactic showdown of unparalleled proportions. The Tuatha Dé Danann, now led by the heroic Lugh, sought to reclaim their sovereignty and secure their place as the rulers of Ireland. Central to this battle was the notorious weapon of Balor, the malevolent eye that could annihilate with a single glance. Lugh, armed with his extraordinary skills and intellect, engaged Balor in a dramatic confrontation. With a well-aimed slingshot, Lugh struck Balor's eye, vanquishing the Fomorian king and decimating their ranks. The Tuatha Dé Danann emerged victorious, securing their dominion over Ireland. The significance of this victory extended far beyond the battlefield; it marked the triumph of order over chaos, wisdom over brute force, and the ascent of the divine over the monstrous.

The Battle of Magh Tuireadh is laden with symbolism and metaphorical significance. It encapsulates the eternal struggle between civilization and the wild, order and chaos, and the divine and the monstrous. The Tuatha Dé Danann's victory reflects the enduring human desire for a world shaped by wisdom, art, and civilization, rather than by primal forces. The battle's legacy reverberates through the annals of Irish mythology, culture, and identity. It embodies the theme of resilience and the capacity of the divine to overcome adversity. In the modern era, it is celebrated as a testament to the enduring spirit of Ireland, a land where myths and legends shape the collective imagination.

The Battle of Magh Tuireadh, as a monumental clash between the Tuatha Dé Danann and the Fomorians, stands as an enduring testament to the richness and complexity of Irish mythology. It is a saga of gods and titans, a narrative that captures the eternal struggle between competing forces and the indomitable spirit of those who seek to shape their destiny. Intricately woven into the fabric of Irish culture, the Battle of Magh Tuireadh transcends its mythic origins to become a symbol of resilience, wisdom, and the enduring power of the human spirit to overcome adversity. It serves as a reminder that the stories of mythology are not merely tales of bygone eras but are living narratives that continue to inspire, captivate, and shape the identity of a nation steeped in the enchantment of its own lore.

The Milesians & The Clash with The Tuatha Dé Danann

The Milesians, also known as the Sons of Míl or Gaels, are a prominent part of Irish mythology and history. Their tale is rich and complex, blending myth and legend with historical elements. Here's an in-depth story about the Milesians of Ireland:

Míl Espáine:

Míl Espáine, whose name is sometimes anglicized as "Milesius," is a central character in the Milesian legend. He is often depicted as a warrior and a leader of the Iberian Celts, living in what is now modern-day Spain. The exact details of his life vary across different versions of the myth, but a few key elements remain consistent:

1. Exile from Iberia: According to some versions of the myth, Míl Espáine was exiled from Iberia due to political strife or conflicts within his own clan. This exile served as the catalyst for his journey to Ireland.
2. The Oracle's Prophecy: Míl Espáine's decision to set sail for Ireland was not arbitrary. In one prominent version of the myth, he had received a prophecy from an oracle that foretold a destiny in Ireland. The oracle's words fueled his determination to reach the Emerald Isle.
3. A Warrior and Leader: Míl Espáine was not merely a wanderer; he was a formidable warrior and leader of his people. His reputation for bravery and military prowess added to the allure of his journey to Ireland.

The Sailing of the Milesians

With a group of loyal followers and family members, Míl Espáine embarked on a legendary voyage across the seas to reach Ireland. The journey was arduous and fraught with challenges, including encounters with storms and other adversities that tested the resolve of the Milesians. The story of Míl Espáine and the Milesians is a fascinating blend of mythology and history. While it is a mythical tale at its core, it reflects the migrations and interactions that occurred in ancient Europe. Some historians suggest that the story of the Milesians may have been inspired by real migrations of Celtic peoples from continental Europe to Ireland, which took place over centuries.

The Arrival in Ireland

When the Milesians finally reached Ireland, they encountered the Tuatha Dé Danann, who had already inhabited the island. This encounter set the stage for the epic Battle of Taillte, a central event in the Milesian saga. Overall, the origins of the Milesians highlight the themes of destiny, migration, and the enduring human quest for a new homeland. While the exact historical accuracy of the Milesian legend is debated, its significance in Irish mythology and its impact on the cultural identity of Ireland cannot be overstated.

The Battle of Taillte

As the Milesians, led by Éire, Amergin, and Éber Finn, arrived at the shores of Ireland, they were met with an eerie silence. The Tuatha Dé Danann, a magical and mystical race who had ruled Ireland for centuries, had been forewarned of their arrival through their druidic powers. A sense of impending conflict hung heavy in the air. Before the battle began, Bres, a half-Fomorian and former king of the Tuatha Dé Danann, stepped forward as an emissary. He offered a peaceful resolution, suggesting that the Milesians should leave Ireland without a fight. Bres argued that Ireland rightfully belonged to the Tuatha Dé Danann. Éire, the queen of the Milesians, rejected Bres's offer, declaring their determination to claim Ireland as their own. The Milesians saw their arrival in Ireland as a fulfillment of destiny and were unwilling to turn back. Amergin, the Milesian druid-poet, invoked a powerful chant, asserting the Milesians' right to the land.

The Battle of Taillte was a climactic showdown that determined the fate of Ireland. The Tuatha Dé Danann, the mythic inhabitants of the island, were known for their powerful magic and supernatural abilities. However, the Milesians were determined to conquer Ireland and claim it as their own, and they brought their own unique strengths to the battlefield. With negotiations failing, the Battle of Taillte erupted in full force. It was a clash of epic proportions. The Tuatha Dé Danann's magic clashed with the Milesians' martial skill. Enchanted weapons met the Milesians' iron swords, and spells collided with Amergin's

incantations. Amergin played a crucial role in the battle. He recited a magical chant that resonated with the land itself, calling upon its elements and spirits to aid the Milesians. His words echoed across the battlefield, invoking the power of the earth, sea, and sky to support his people.
The Tuatha Dé Danann were skilled in various forms of magic, from shape-shifting to control over the elements. During the battle, they unleashed powerful storms, summoned mystical creatures, and used illusions to disorient the Milesian warriors. The battlefields themselves were transformed, with the very landscape becoming a weapon in the hands of the Tuatha Dé Danann.

Amergin, one of the Milesian leaders, was not just a warrior but also a druid and a poet. He possessed great wisdom and knowledge of the land. Amergin's knowledge allowed him to counteract the magical defenses of the Tuatha Dé Danann. He recited a powerful incantation, known as the "Song of Amergin," which established a spiritual connection between the Milesians and the land, making their presence in Ireland undeniable. The Battle of Taillte was not solely determined by the strength of arms. Mythology suggests that divine forces were at play. The goddess Ériu, after whom Ireland is named, appeared to the Milesians and declared her support for their cause. This divine intervention provided the Milesians with both moral and supernatural encouragement.

The Turning Point: As the battle raged on, it became clear that the Milesians were gaining the upper hand. The Tuatha Dé Danann's magic began to wane, and their forces dwindled. The realization that their ancient magical powers were no longer enough to hold onto Ireland led to a sense of inevitability. Throughout the battle, it became clear that the Tuatha Dé Danann's magic alone could not secure their victory. Sensing defeat, they made a fateful decision. Rather than facing total annihilation, they chose to retreat to the Otherworld, where their magic could continue to thrive.

Milesian Victory and the Claiming of Ireland
With the Tuatha Dé Danann's retreat, the Milesians emerged victorious at the Battle of Taillte. They had won the right to rule over Ireland, although the memory of the magical conflict with the Tuatha Dé Danann would forever be etched into Irish folklore. The Battle of Taillte

symbolizes the clash between the old mystical world of the Tuatha Dé Danann and the arrival of the Milesians, who brought with them a new era in Irish history. It's a story of power, destiny, and the changing of the guard in the mythic history of Ireland.

The victory of the Milesians in the Battle of Taillte is a central theme in Irish mythology and history. It symbolizes the transition from the mythic and magical era of the Tuatha Dé Danann to a more mortal and historical period in Ireland. It also underscores the enduring connection between the Irish people and the land. The Milesians' victory laid the foundation for the subsequent history and culture of Ireland, marking the beginning of the Gaelic and Celtic influence on the island. The story of their triumph continues to be celebrated in Irish folklore, poetry, and song, ensuring that their legacy endures in the hearts and minds of the Irish people.

The Division of Ireland by the Milesians

After their victory over the Tuatha Dé Danann and the establishment of their rule in Ireland, the Milesians divided the land into two main kingdoms, effectively splitting the island into north and south. This division was not just a geographical one; it also had cultural and political implications. Éber Finn and Éremon, two of the Milesian leaders, each ruled one of these divided territories. Éber Finn claimed the northern part of Ireland, while Éremon took control of the southern region. This division wasn't marked by hostility but rather by a recognition of their respective leadership roles. Éire, the wife of Amergin, played a symbolic role in this division. Her name was used to refer to the entire island of Ireland. This not only reflected her importance in the mythology but also symbolized the unity of the land under the rule of the Milesians. Her name, Éire, has remained as the poetic and historical name for Ireland in the Irish language.

Cultural and Regional Distinctions

The division of Ireland into north and south also laid the groundwork for regional distinctions in the country's culture and history. Over time, different kingdoms, clans, and regions developed their own unique identities and histories. This division helped shape the rich tapestry of Irish culture and regional traditions. While the division of Ireland by the Milesians is primarily a mythological narrative, it has historical significance as well. It reflects the political landscape of ancient Ireland, where various regional kingdoms and clans coexisted and sometimes clashed. This early division laid the groundwork for the complex history of Ireland's political divisions and conflicts in later centuries.

In modern times, the division of Ireland by the Milesians remains a part of Irish cultural heritage. It is often cited as one of the early events that contributed to the diverse and multifaceted nature of Irish identity. The concept of Éire as the poetic name for Ireland continues to be cherished, and the north-south division serves as a historical backdrop to contemporary discussions about Irish history and politics.

The division of Ireland by the Milesians represents not only a geographical split but also the beginnings of regional and cultural distinctions within the island. This division has had a lasting impact on Ireland's history, culture, and identity, making it a crucial element of the country's mythology and heritage.

The Legacy of the Milesians

The Milesians are considered the legendary ancestors of the Irish people. This connection forms a vital part of Irish identity, fostering a sense of heritage and continuity that has endured for millennia. Many Irish families and clans trace their lineage back to the Milesians, and this ancestral link is often a source of pride and identity. The Milesians brought with them Celtic culture and language, which had a profound and lasting impact on Ireland. Their arrival marked a significant shift in the island's cultural landscape, influencing art, music, folklore, and religious practices. The Celts' distinctive artistic styles, including intricate metalwork and ornate knotwork designs, continue to be celebrated in contemporary Irish culture. The Gaelic language, rooted in Celtic traditions, is the primary language of Ireland. The Milesians played a pivotal role in the spread and preservation of the Gaelic language. Today, the Irish language, or Gaeilge, is still spoken and studied, and efforts to promote its use and preservation are ongoing.

The stories and legends surrounding the Milesians, particularly their battles with the Tuatha Dé Danann, have provided a rich source of inspiration for Irish folklore and literature. These myths have been passed down through generations and continue to influence contemporary Irish literature, from the works of Yeats to modern fantasy writers. Many place names in Ireland have their origins in the Milesian mythology. Éire, the Irish name for Ireland, is a direct reference to Éire, one of the Milesian queens. Additionally, many geographical features, rivers, and landmarks are linked to the events and figures in Milesian lore, reinforcing the deep connection between myth and landscape. Elements of Milesian mythology have found their way into national symbols and emblems. The harp, for example, has been a symbol of Ireland for centuries and is often associated with the legendary harp of Dagda, a Tuatha Dé Danann figure from the Milesian myths. The harp is featured on Ireland's coat of arms and currency. The legacy of the Milesians is celebrated through various cultural events and traditions in Ireland. St. Patrick's Day, a global celebration of Irish culture, is one such occasion. The tales of the Milesians are also retold and commemorated in festivals, storytelling, and cultural events throughout the year. The Milesians are a testament to the enduring spirit of the Irish people, as their story reflects a history of resilience, perseverance, and the pursuit of a homeland. This historical identity continues to shape the Irish character and informs how the Irish view themselves in relation to their history and heritage.

In summary, the legacy of the Milesians is deeply interwoven into the fabric of Irish culture and history. Their mythical journey to Ireland, their cultural contributions, and their role as ancestral figures continue to inspire and connect generations of Irish people to their rich and storied past.

The Historical Context
1. *Celtic Migration:* The story of the Milesians is often associated with the arrival of the Celts in Ireland. While the exact timeline and nature of this migration are subjects of debate among historians and archaeologists, it is widely accepted that the Celts, an Indo-European people, began migrating into Ireland and other parts of Europe around 500 BCE. The Milesians are sometimes seen as symbolic of this broader Celtic migration.
2. *Cultural Exchange:* The Milesians are traditionally portrayed as warriors, and their arrival in Ireland is symbolic of a cultural and linguistic exchange. The Celts brought with them a distinct language (Goidelic or Q-Celtic), artistic styles, metalworking techniques, and religious beliefs. This Celtic culture gradually assimilated with the existing culture of Ireland, which had been influenced by earlier inhabitants like the Tuatha Dé Danann.

3. *Influence on Irish Language and Culture:* The introduction of the Goidelic language by the Milesians eventually gave rise to the Irish language (Gaeilge). Today, the Irish language is still spoken in parts of Ireland and has a deep cultural significance. It has also influenced the names of places and people in Ireland, as well as Irish literature and folklore.
4. *The Concept of Sovereignty:* The Milesian arrival is intertwined with the concept of sovereignty in Irish mythology. Éire, the personification of Ireland, played a central role in their mythology. The Milesians sought to marry her to legitimize their rule. This concept of a divine or symbolic marriage between rulers and the land is a recurring theme in Irish mythology and reflects the importance of the land in the culture.
5. *The Transition from Myth to History:* While the story of the Milesians is rooted in mythology, it marks a transition from purely mythical narratives to more historical accounts. The introduction of the Milesians is sometimes seen as a way to reconcile the mythological origins of Ireland with the historical reality of Celtic migrations.
6. *Modern Identity and Nationalism:* The Milesian myth has been used to reinforce a sense of Irish identity and nationalism. In the 19th and early 20th centuries, during the Irish cultural revival and struggle for independence, this myth was invoked to connect the Irish people with their ancient heritage and assert their right to self-determination.

In summary, the historical context of the Milesians is complex, blending mythology, archaeology, and historical interpretations. Their arrival in Ireland represents a pivotal moment in the island's history, marking the beginning of significant cultural and linguistic changes that continue to shape Ireland's identity to this day.

Modern Significance

The tale of the Milesians plays a vital role in shaping the cultural identity of Ireland. It reinforces the idea that the Irish people have a long and storied history rooted in myth and legend. This shared cultural narrative helps foster a sense of belonging and pride among the Irish population, both at home and in the global Irish diaspora.

During the struggle for Irish independence in the 19th and early 20th centuries, the Milesians' story became a symbol of resistance and self-determination. It was used to rally the Irish people against British rule, emphasizing the idea that Ireland should be ruled by its own people, just as the Milesians sought to claim the island as their own.

The myth of the Milesians has had a profound influence on Irish literature and language. Many renowned Irish writers, including W.B.

Yeats, Lady Augusta Gregory, and James Joyce, drew inspiration from Irish mythology, weaving its themes and characters into their works. This literary heritage continues to shape Irish literature and artistic expression. The Milesian mythology has contributed to Ireland's thriving tourism industry. Visitors are drawn to the rich tapestry of Irish folklore and history, and many historical sites, such as Tara and Newgrange, are associated with the Milesians and the ancient tales of Ireland. This cultural tourism brings economic benefits to the country.

Festivals and Celebrations

Irish culture celebrates its mythology and history through various festivals and events. St. Patrick's Day, for example, often incorporates elements of Irish mythology, including the Milesians, in parades and festivities. These celebrations help keep the ancient stories alive in the modern consciousness. The Milesian narrative also serves as a subject of academic study. Scholars and researchers explore the historical and cultural aspects of the story, shedding light on its origins and evolution. This academic interest contributes to a deeper understanding of Irish heritage. The Milesians' journey and eventual victory over the Tuatha Dé Danann symbolize themes of unity and solidarity, transcending divisions and conflicts. In a modern context, the story can be seen as a reminder of the importance of unity among the diverse people of Ireland, regardless of regional or political differences.

In summary, the story of the Milesians is more than just a myth; it is a foundational element of Irish culture and identity. Its modern significance extends to various aspects of Irish life, from art and literature to politics and tourism, making it an integral part of Ireland's past and present.

Chapter 6
The Tuatha Dé Danann and Their Enduring Connection to Irish Landmarks

The Tuatha Dé Danann, revered as divine beings in Irish mythology, maintain a profound and enduring connection with the landscape of Ireland. Their presence is interwoven with famous Irish locations, landmarks, and sites, imbuing these places with mythic significance and cultural depth. Among the many sites associated with the Tuatha Dé Danann, two prominent examples are Newgrange and the Hill of Tara. These sites not only serve as testaments to the rich tapestry of Irish myth but also evoke the eternal allure of Ireland's mystical past.

Newgrange: Portal to the Otherworld

Newgrange, one of Ireland's most iconic megalithic monuments, stands as a testament to the Tuatha Dé Danann's mythic legacy. Located in County Meath, Newgrange is a neolithic passage tomb constructed over 5,000 years ago. Its architectural precision and alignment with the winter solstice sunrise indicate a deep understanding of astronomy and the cyclical nature of life and death. In Irish mythology, Newgrange is often associated with Aengus Óg, one of the Tuatha Dé Danann, renowned for his connection to love and youth. According to legend, Aengus lived at Newgrange, where he pursued his love interest, Caer Ibormeith, who took the form of a swan. This connection between Aengus and Newgrange symbolizes the timeless themes of love and transformation, mirroring the passage tomb's function as a portal to the Otherworld—a realm of myth and magic.

The structure's inner chamber, adorned with intricate carvings and stones from various regions of Ireland, reflects the Tuatha Dé Danann's reverence for art and craftsmanship. Newgrange's enduring presence as both an architectural marvel and a vessel of myth exemplifies the intersection of Irish history, culture, and mythology.

The Hill of Tara: Seat of the High Kings
The Hill of Tara, situated in the picturesque County Meath, holds a place of unparalleled significance in the mythic tapestry of Irish history. Revered as the foremost sacred site linked to the illustrious Tuatha Dé Danann, Tara transcends mere geography; it embodies the heart and soul of ancient Irish heritage.

Nestled within the lush landscapes of County Meath, Tara's eminence extends from the ethereal to the earthly. It serves as the hallowed ground where the High Kings of Ireland, chosen by the Tuatha Dé Danann themselves, ascended to their thrones. This crowning ceremony was no ordinary affair but a ritual laden with divine purpose, a sacred dance between the mortal realm and the Otherworld.

Atop Tara's rolling hills, the Tuatha Dé Danann convened their courts, establishing it as the veritable nucleus of their celestial governance. This elevated terrain, where the mundane and the mystical converged, resonated with the echoes of ancient wisdom and mythic power. It was here that the Tuatha Dé Danann wielded their authority, shaping the destinies of both mortals and immortals alike.

As the epicenter of their influence, Tara symbolizes the Tuatha Dé Danann's enduring connection to the land and its people. The legends that swirl around this sacred hill attest to its pivotal role in the Irish saga, bridging the realms of history and myth, and forever enshrining the Tuatha Dé Danann in the annals of Irish folklore.

Brú na Bóinne: The World Heritage Site
Brú na Bóinne, a UNESCO World Heritage Site nestled in County Meath, Ireland, is a realm of profound historical and mythological significance. Here, the hallowed earth cradles the enigmatic passage tombs of Newgrange, Knowth, and Dowth, each a testament to the ancient mastery of our ancestors. But what sets Brú na Bóinne apart from mere archaeological wonders is its deep-rooted connection with Irish mythology. In the rich tapestry of Irish folklore, these tombs resonate as sacred resting places, entwined with the legends of the Tuatha Dé Danann, the divine beings of ancient Ireland's pantheon.

Legend whispers that within the chambers of Newgrange, Knowth, and Dowth lie the mortal remains of revered figures from the Tuatha Dé Danann. These ethereal beings, possessed of extraordinary power and wisdom, are said to have once walked the verdant landscapes of Ireland.

As the sun casts its first rays upon the imposing entrance of Newgrange during the winter solstice, a testament to the ancient builders' astronomical prowess, one can't help but feel the presence of these mythical deities. It's as if the stones themselves resonate with the echoes of the Tuatha Dé Danann, connecting the mortal world to the realm of the divine. So, when we stand before the megalithic wonders of Brú na Bóinne, we do more than admire the craftsmanship of our ancestors; we enter a realm where history and myth converge. It's a place where the spirits of gods and goddesses of old linger, reminding us that the past is woven into the very fabric of Ireland's ancient landscapes.

Lough Neagh: The Twelve Chief Lough of Ireland
Lough Neagh, located in Northern Ireland, proudly holds the title of being the largest lake on the island of Ireland. However, its origins are steeped in the enchanting lore of the Tuatha Dé Danann, a mystical and powerful race of beings from Irish mythology. According to the ancient tales, this vast body of water owes its existence to the otherworldly craftsmanship of the Tuatha Dé Danann, brought to life through the magical mastery of their chief Druid, Máel Dúin. The creation of Lough Neagh, as the myths tell, is a testament to the heart-wrenching beauty and sorrow that often intertwine in the world of gods and goddesses. It is said that this magnificent lake was formed from the very tears of a goddess named Ériu. Her weeping, a poignant reflection of some divine heartache, contributed to the shaping of this remarkable landscape.

In the annals of Irish mythology, Ériu is one of the matron goddesses, closely associated with the land itself, representing the sovereignty of Ireland. Her tears, shed for reasons hidden in the annals of myth, are believed to have flowed into the earth, creating the vast expanse of Lough Neagh. This connection between the goddess Ériu, her tears, and the creation of the lake endows Lough Neagh with profound significance in the Tuatha Dé Danann's rich and intricate tapestry of legends.

This enduring mythological link between Lough Neagh and the Tuatha Dé Danann adds a layer of mystique and wonder to this natural wonder of Northern Ireland. It serves as a reminder of the deep intertwining of the supernatural and the natural in the folklore and legends of the Emerald Isle.

The Paps of Anu: The Breasts of Anu

The Paps of Anu, also known as the Dá Chích Anann, stand proudly in the picturesque landscape of County Kerry. These striking twin mountains hold a profound connection to the ancient Irish mythology of the Tuatha Dé Danann, intricately tied to the enigmatic figure of Anu, the revered mother goddess. Rising majestically from the lush, rolling hills, the Paps of Anu are named as a tribute to Anu herself, a deity celebrated for her association with fertility and boundless abundance. In the intricate tapestry of Irish folklore, her name resonates as a symbol of life's nourishing and sustaining aspects.

Anu's significance within the realm of the Tuatha Dé Danann is captivating. These divine beings, the "People of the Goddess Danu," are renowned for their supernatural powers, wisdom, and their role as the foundational mythological ancestors of Ireland. Anu, as a mother goddess, symbolizes the life force and vitality that flows through the very land upon which the Paps of Anu proudly stand. The name "Anu" evokes the lush, bountiful essence of the land, echoing the fertility that sustains both the earthly and mystical realms. Her presence intertwines with the Tuatha Dé Danann's stories and myths, highlighting the deep spiritual connection between the land, its people, and the divine.

As you stand before the Paps of Anu, you can't help but feel the echoes of ancient tales, where gods and goddesses once walked the emerald fields of Ireland. These Twin Peaks, reaching for the heavens, serve as a reminder of the enduring bond between the Tuatha Dé Danann and the nurturing essence of Anu, the mother of prosperity.

Slieve League Cliffs: The Mountain of Stone Pillars

Slieve League Cliffs, the magnificent coastal wonders of County Donegal, hold a mystical connection to the Tuatha Dé Danann, particularly through their association with Manannán mac Lir, the revered sea god of Irish mythology. These towering cliffs, which rise majestically from the wild Atlantic, become an enchanting backdrop to the tales of ancient Ireland. At the heart of this connection lies Manannán mac Lir, a pivotal figure among the Tuatha Dé Danann, known for his guardianship of the coastline and dominion over the seas. As the waves crash against the rugged cliffs, it's as if Manannán himself, with his deep connection to the waters, watches over this dramatic landscape.

These cliffs, among the highest in Europe, seem to bear witness to the timeless tales of the Tuatha Dé Danann. Legends tell of Manannán's role in protecting the land and sea, ensuring their harmonious coexistence. As the god of the sea, he safeguarded seafarers and the mystical realms beyond the horizon, bridging the mortal world with the Otherworld, a realm of enchantment and magic often associated with the Tuatha Dé Danann. The sheer grandeur and natural beauty of Slieve League Cliffs, with their sheer drops and windswept heights, evoke the same sense of awe and wonder inspired by the Tuatha Dé Danann themselves. Just as the Tuatha Dé Danann were considered deities of exceptional skill, magic, and wisdom, these cliffs exude an otherworldly charm that seems to transcend the ordinary, drawing visitors into a realm of myth and mysticism.

Whether gazing out to sea from the precipice of Slieve League or exploring the rugged terrain below, one can't help but feel the presence of the Tuatha Dé Danann, especially Manannán mac Lir, whose spirit lingers in the crashing waves and the whispering winds that echo through these timeless cliffs. Slieve League Cliffs serve as a testament to the enduring bond between Ireland's natural wonders and its rich mythological heritage, where the lines between the mundane and the magical are beautifully blurred.

The Burren: The Rocky District
The Burren, located in the captivating County Clare, boasts a landscape as unique as it is mysterious. Nestled within its rocky expanse lies a connection to the mythological past of Ireland, specifically to the realm of the Tuatha Dé Danann. The heart of this remarkable region is intertwined with the legend of Aoife, the queen of the Tuatha Dé Danann. According to ancient lore, she made her home amidst the limestone labyrinth that is The Burren. The name "Aoife" itself holds an air of ethereality, echoing through the ages as a symbol of divine presence. Her story is one of grace and power, traits that resonate throughout the landscape she purportedly inhabited.

The Burren's enigmatic terrain, often likened to an otherworldly tapestry, has led to a tantalizing connection between this earthly realm and the mystical abode of the Tuatha Dé Danann. Some perceive The Burren as a portal, a physical reflection of the elusive Otherworld, where the Tuatha Dé Danann are said to reside. The juxtaposition of rugged limestone pavements, peculiar karst formations, and an array of rare flora paints a surreal picture, mirroring the fantastical realm of Irish mythology.

It is in this surreal landscape that the Tuatha Dé Danann's presence feels most tangible, where the boundary between the mortal realm and the divine is blurred. As you explore The Burren's hauntingly beautiful vistas, one can't help but wonder if Aoife and her celestial kin left an indelible mark on this captivating land, making it a living testament to Ireland's mythical heritage.

Cú Chulainn's Castle: A Key Ancient Site in Ireland
Cú Chulainn's Castle, also known as Dunseverick Castle (not to be confused with Cú Chulainn's Castle located in Dundalk, Co Louth), stands as a striking testament to the rich tapestry of Irish mythology, particularly its connection to the legendary warrior Cú Chulainn and his interactions with the enigmatic Tuatha Dé Danann. This coastal stronghold, situated in the breathtaking County Antrim of Northern Ireland, becomes a nexus where the threads of myth and reality are intricately woven together. It was amidst these dramatic coastal panoramas that Cú Chulainn, a figure of unparalleled renown in Irish folklore, is said to have established his own bastion – Cú Chulainn's

Castle. In this remarkable setting, the boundaries between the earthly realm and the mystical dimensions inhabited by the Tuatha Dé Danann appear to blur, giving rise to tales that seamlessly meld the historical and the mystical.

Within the stout stone walls of Dunseverick Castle, a veritable tapestry of legends unfolds. Here, Cú Chulainn's heroic exploits intersect with encounters with the Tuatha Dé Danann, the ancient gods of Ireland. These narratives often unfold in ways that transcend the ordinary, where the veil between humanity and the divine grows thin, affording moments of astonishment, wonder, and even trepidation. In the backdrop of this imposing castle, clinging steadfastly to the cliffs, one can almost envision Cú Chulainn locking blades with these ethereal beings, forging alliances or facing trials that test his indomitable spirit. This location, steeped in history and myth, becomes the very crossroads where the mystical and corporeal realms converge. It's a place where the enduring legacy of Cú Chulainn and the mysterious Tuatha Dé Danann continues to captivate the imagination of those drawn to the mysteries of Irish mythology.

These landmarks are not mere relics of the past; they are living symbols of Ireland's enduring connection to its mythic heritage. They remind us that the stories of the Tuatha Dé Danann, like the landscape itself, are woven into the very fabric of Irish culture, history, and identity. In exploring these sites, we embark on a journey through time and myth, where the ancient gods continue to whisper their tales to those who seek to listen.

These connections between the Tuatha Dé Danann and Irish landmarks add an enchanting layer to Ireland's cultural and mythological heritage. They blend the natural beauty of the land with the imaginative tales of its ancient inhabitants, leaving a lasting impression on both the landscape and the folklore of the Emerald Isle.

Chapter 7
Otherworldly Realms

Understanding the concept of the Otherworld in Celtic mythology

Celtic mythology is interwoven with a captivating array of supernatural beings, heroic feats, and mystical realms. Among these realms, the concept of the Otherworld stands as a pivotal and enchanting element. A realm shrouded in mystery, the Otherworld serves as a bridge between the mortal realm and the divine, holding deep significance in the beliefs and narratives of the Celts. This chapter aims to explore the intricate concept of the Otherworld in Celtic mythology, shedding light on its characteristics, importance, and enduring influence.

The Nature of the Otherworld

In Celtic mythology, the Otherworld is often portrayed as a parallel dimension, a place that exists alongside the mortal world but remains hidden from ordinary human perception. It is a realm beyond the confines of time and space, where supernatural beings reside and where the laws of nature are governed by a different set of rules. The Otherworld is characterized by its ethereal landscapes, enchanting landscapes, and a sense of timelessness that contrasts sharply with the mortal realm. The inhabitants of the Otherworld play a crucial role in Celtic myths and legends. These inhabitants include deities, faeries, spirits, and other mythical creatures. Notable among them are the Tuatha Dé Danann. The Otherworldly beings often possess powers that far surpass those of humans, and interactions with them often lead to transformative experiences or tests of character for mortals.

Role in Celtic Mythology

The Otherworld serves as a backdrop for many significant events in Celtic mythology. It is a realm of both challenges and rewards, where heroes venture to prove their worth or to seek knowledge, treasures, or healing. Often, mortal characters are drawn into the Otherworld through dreams, visions, or portals, embarking on quests that test their courage and resourcefulness. The Otherworldly adventures contribute to the theme of transformation and personal growth, where characters return to the mortal realm changed by their experiences.

The Otherworld in Celtic mythology carries profound symbolic meaning. It represents the liminal space between life and death, the known and the unknown, and the mundane and the divine. This duality underscores the interconnectedness of existence and the belief that the boundaries between realms are porous. The Otherworld also embodies the idea of cyclical renewal, as characters who journey into it often return with renewed perspectives and abilities.

The Otherworld in Modern Context

The concept of the Otherworld continues to captivate contemporary audiences, leaving its mark on literature, art, and pop culture. Fantasy novels, films, and video games often draw inspiration from Celtic mythology, integrating the concept of the Otherworld into their narratives. The enchantment of the Otherworld resonates with our innate human curiosity about the unknown and our desire to explore realms beyond the ordinary.

The Otherworld stands as a captivating and enigmatic element within Celtic mythology. It is a realm that transcends the ordinary, offering a space for encounters with the divine, tests of character, and transformative experiences. Its enduring influence in both ancient myths and modern adaptations speaks to its timeless allure. The concept of the Otherworld continues to be a window into the Celtic worldview, inviting us to contemplate the mysteries that lie beyond the tangible realm and to consider the intricate connections between mortal and divine dimensions.

Sidhe: The mystical realm of the Tuatha Dé Danann

The concept of the Otherworld holds a special place, offering a glimpse into a realm beyond the mortal world. At the heart of this Otherworldly tapestry lies the Sidhe, a mystical domain intricately intertwined with the Tuatha Dé Danann, the divine race of Irish mythology. The Sidhe is more than a mere setting; it is a realm of enchantment, beauty, and wonder, a place where gods, spirits, and mortals intertwine. We will delve into the depths of the Sidhe, exploring its characteristics, connections to the Tuatha Dé Danann, and its enduring influence on Irish culture and storytelling.

The Sidhe: Gateway to Another Realm

The term "Sidhe" (pronounced "shee") translates to "mounds" or "hills" in Irish, often referring to ancient burial mounds or barrows. However, in the context of Irish mythology, it signifies more than geographical features; it represents a supernatural realm existing parallel to the mortal world. The Sidhe is a realm of liminality, where time and space hold different meanings, and reality blends with the magical and the mystical. The Tuatha Dé Danann, as divine beings, are often associated with the Sidhe. According to mythology, they are said to have retreated to this realm after the Battle of Magh Tuireadh, where they secured victory over the Fomorians. The Sidhe serves as a haven for these gods and goddesses, a place where their powers and knowledge can thrive. Within its enchanted hills, they continue to influence the mortal realm, occasionally interacting with humans or crossing over into their world.

Characteristics of the Sidhe

The Sidhe is characterized by its ethereal beauty and otherworldly atmosphere. It's often depicted as a realm of perpetual twilight or as a place untouched by time, where nature and architecture blend seamlessly. The Sidhe's landscapes are often described as idyllic, with lush meadows, crystal-clear lakes, and magnificent gardens. Ancient stone circles, megaliths, and enigmatic structures are scattered throughout the realm, reflecting the advanced knowledge and craftsmanship of the Tuatha Dé Danann. The boundary between the Sidhe and the mortal world is not always rigid. There are instances in mythology where individuals from both realms interact. Mortals occasionally find themselves drawn into the Otherworld, sometimes through the haunting sound of faerie music or the allure of a Sidhe mound. These interactions often lead to unexpected outcomes, with mortals returning to the human world to find that years have passed, even though only moments were spent in the Sidhe.

Cultural Impact and Legacy
The influence of the Sidhe extends beyond the realm of mythology. Its allure has captivated generations, inspiring poets, writers, and artists. The concept of the Sidhe has deeply rooted itself in Irish cultural identity, shaping stories, folklore, and traditions. Faerie folktales often feature Sidhe inhabitants, portraying them as both benevolent and capricious beings. Additionally, the Sidhe has contributed to the mystique of Ireland's landscape, with certain places believed to be portals to the Otherworld.

In the intricate tapestry of Irish mythology, the Sidhe emerges as a realm of magic and mystery, a place where gods and mortals intersect and where the fantastical becomes tangible. Its association with the Tuatha Dé Danann adds depth to the stories of these divine beings, showcasing their influence on both the mortal world and the Otherworld. As the Sidhe continues to cast its enchanting spell, it perpetuates the legacy of the Tuatha Dé Danann, reminding us of the enduring power of myth, magic, and the uncharted realms that lie beyond our perception.

Chapter 8
Symbolism and Themes

The connections between the mortal and Otherworldly realms in Celtic mythology carry symbolic meanings and themes. The interactions emphasize the cyclical nature of life, death, and rebirth. Mortals who enter the Otherworld often find that time operates differently there, leading to stories of individuals who return after what feels like a short visit, only to discover that many years have passed in the mortal realm. This cyclic aspect reflects the interconnectedness of the realms and the concept of eternity. Additionally, the Otherworld is often associated with concepts of wisdom, healing, and rejuvenation. The Tuatha Dé Danann, with their advanced knowledge and magical abilities, exemplify these qualities. The interactions between the realms provide mortals with the opportunity to gain insight, inspiration, and sometimes even transformation.

The concept of Otherworldly realms and their connections to the mortal world are fundamental to understanding Celtic mythology and the stories of the Tuatha Dé Danann. These connections highlight the intertwining of the magical and the mundane, the known and the unknown. The Tuatha Dé Danann's interactions with mortals and their influence on human affairs underscore the belief that these realms are not separate, but are part of a larger cosmic tapestry. Exploring the Otherworldly connections enriches our understanding of the complexities of Celtic mythology and the enduring allure of the Tuatha Dé Danann's stories.

Themes of heroism, sacrifice, and destiny
In Irish mythology, the tales of the Tuatha Dé Danann are woven with intricate threads of symbolism and themes that resonate deeply with the human experience. Among the most prominent of these themes are heroism, sacrifice, and destiny. These themes intertwine throughout the stories of the Tuatha Dé Danann, reflecting their divine struggles and profound connections to the mortal world. Heroism, a timeless concept that transcends cultures, takes center stage in the stories of the Tuatha Dé Danann. The gods and goddesses of this divine pantheon are often portrayed as heroic figures who exhibit exceptional courage, strength, and resilience in the face of daunting challenges. The epitome of this

heroism is embodied by figures such as Nuada, the king with the silver arm, and Lugh, the multi-skilled god.

Sacrifice: The Price of Divine Duty
Sacrifice, another profound theme within the Tuatha Dé Danann narratives, underscores the complexity of the gods' relationships with both mortals and their own kind. Nuada's sacrifice of his arm for the greater good of his people symbolizes the selflessness and commitment that leaders and heroes often must embody. His physical sacrifice for the preservation of his kingship serves as a poignant reminder that leadership comes with responsibilities that demand personal sacrifices. The theme of sacrifice is further exemplified by the death of Nuada in the Battle of Magh Tuireadh. His ultimate sacrifice on the battlefield illustrates the depth of his commitment to his people's welfare. This act of self-sacrifice adds a layer of poignancy to his character and contributes to the overarching theme of the divine duty to protect and guide the mortal world.

Destiny: Threads Woven by Fate
Destiny weaves its intricate threads throughout the mythology of the Tuatha Dé Danann, shaping the lives of both gods and mortals alike. The concept of fate, often intertwined with the Otherworldly realm where the Tuatha Dé Danann reside, underscores the idea that their actions are part of a greater cosmic design. Lugh's destiny, for instance, intertwines with his heroic journey and his eventual role as a leader, a destiny he embraces with courage and determination. Nuada's journey, from the loss of his arm to his final sacrifice, mirrors the idea that destiny can be both challenging and transformative. His journey is an embodiment of the hero's path, marked by trials that lead to self-discovery and eventual transcendence.

The themes of heroism, sacrifice, and destiny within the tales of the Tuatha Dé Danann delve deep into the human psyche, exploring the complexities of leadership, personal growth, and the interconnectedness of divine and mortal realms. These themes resonate across time and cultures, reminding us that the struggles and triumphs of gods and heroes mirror our own. Through their stories, the Tuatha Dé Danann continue to inspire reflection on the enduring qualities that define our shared humanity.

Chapter 9
Magic, Craftsmanship, and Skills

Crafting and magical prowess of the Tuatha Dé Danann
The Tuatha Dé Danann, a divine and enigmatic group of beings from Irish mythology, are renowned not only for their divine lineage and heroic exploits but also for their exceptional magical abilities, unparalleled craftsmanship, and diverse skills. This chapter delves into the intricate tapestry of magic and craftsmanship woven by the Tuatha Dé Danann, uncovering their contributions to Irish mythology and culture.

1. *Mastery of Magic:* The Tuatha Dé Danann were imbued with magical prowess that set them apart from ordinary mortals. Their command over various forms of magic was instrumental in their battles, interactions, and daily lives.

This mastery was demonstrated through:
- Shape-shifting: The ability to transform into animals or other forms.
- Elemental control: Manipulation of natural elements like fire, water, and wind.
- Illusion and glamour: Casting spells to create illusions or conceal their true forms.
- Healing magic: Dian Cecht's healing arts and Nuada's silver arm are emblematic examples.

2. *Artisanal Excellence:* The Tuatha Dé Danann were unparalleled craftsmen, known for their exquisite creations that combined artistry with magical attributes:
- The Cauldron of the Dagda: A magical cauldron capable of providing unlimited sustenance, symbolizing abundance and generosity.
- The Spear of Lugh: A formidable weapon representing Lugh's warrior skills and the mastery of craftsmanship.
- Ogma's Ogham: The invention of Ogham script, a magical writing system that encoded knowledge and wisdom.

3. *Nuada's Silver Arm:* Nuada's silver arm is a prime example of both craftsmanship and magic among the Tuatha Dé Danann. Crafted by Dian Cecht, this functional replacement for his lost hand was a fusion of medical skill and enchantment. The arm's ability to function as a normal

limb while being forged from silver symbolized the harmonious union of technology and magic.

4. *Lia Fáil:* The Lia Fáil, or "Stone of Destiny," showcased the Tuatha Dé Danann's connection to both magic and kingship. As the ancient coronation stone of Irish kings, the Lia Fáil possessed magical qualities, resonating with the rightful ruler's voice upon their coronation, symbolizing the union of divine mandate and earthly authority.

5. *The Role of Craftsmanship:* Craftsmanship among the Tuatha Dé Danann was not limited to weapons and tools. Their creations often held symbolic meanings and reflected their values:
- Dagda's harp, which could control emotions and seasons, reflected the intertwining of music, magic, and nature.
- The ornate architecture of the Otherworld, believed to be designed by the Tuatha Dé Danann, showcased their fusion of aesthetic beauty and magical properties.

6. *Legacy and Influence:* The magical and artisanal legacy of the Tuatha Dé Danann continues to influence Irish culture:
- The integration of magic and craftsmanship in Irish folklore, where their creations and abilities often reappear.
- The enduring fascination with magical items like cauldrons, swords, and harps in contemporary Irish literature and art.

7. *Spiritual Connection and Cosmic Balance:* The Tuatha Dé Danann's magic and craftsmanship went beyond mere feats of power; they were deeply interconnected with the spiritual fabric of the universe. Their actions maintained cosmic balance and sustained the harmony between mortal and divine realms:
- Nuada's role as a just and wise king, balancing mortal and divine concerns, showcased the Tuatha Dé Danann's commitment to maintaining equilibrium.
- Lugh's multi-faceted abilities exemplified the integration of diverse skills, mirroring the intricate web of magic and craftsmanship that characterized their society.

8. *Crafting Beyond the Physical:* The Tuatha Dé Danann's craftsmanship extended beyond tangible objects, encompassing intangible aspects of life and culture:

- Their creation of myths and legends added to the collective consciousness, shaping cultural narratives that endure to this day.
- Their manipulation of elements and energies underscored their role as guardians of natural forces, reinforcing their divine stewardship.

9. *Transformation and Evolution:* The Tuatha Dé Danann's magic and craftsmanship also symbolize the concept of transformation and evolution:
- The motif of shape-shifting reflects their adaptability and willingness to change when circumstances demand it.
- Their ability to bridge the mortal and Otherworldly realms signifies their role as intermediaries between different planes of existence.

10. *Moral Complexity and Ethical Dilemmas:* The Tuatha Dé Danann's magical abilities and craftsmanship weren't devoid of moral complexities:
- Nuada's loss of his arm and the subsequent crafting of the silver arm raise questions about the ethics of using magic to overcome physical limitations.
- The Tuatha Dé Danann's involvement in conflicts and battles sparks debates about the responsibility that comes with wielding powerful magic.
-

11. *Modern Interpretations and Reflections:* Contemporary literature, art, and media continue to draw inspiration from the Tuatha Dé Danann's magic and craftsmanship:
- Authors and creators reimagine their stories, exploring the interplay between magic, technology, and humanity in the modern world.
- Artists depict their craftsmanship as an allegory for the intricate balance between humanity and nature, echoing the Tuatha Dé Danann's connection to both.

12. *The Legacy of Enchantment:* The legacy of the Tuatha Dé Danann's magic and craftsmanship extends far beyond the pages of mythology:
- Their enchanting tales inspire readers to explore the boundaries of human potential, encouraging creativity, imagination, and innovation.
- Their ethos of using magical talents and skills for the betterment of society invites us to reflect on how we can utilize our own strengths to create positive change.

The Tuatha Dé Danann's remarkable blend of magic and craftsmanship underscores their divine nature and enduring impact on Irish mythology. Their skills in shaping reality through magic and forging extraordinary creations demonstrate the intricate interplay between the mystical and the material. By unraveling the threads of their magical and artisanal accomplishments, we gain a deeper understanding of their cultural significance and the enchanting tapestry of Irish mythology.

In summation, the magic, craftsmanship, and skills of the Tuatha Dé Danann are a testament to the intricate relationship between the mortal and the divine, the tangible and the intangible. As we unravel the threads of their abilities, we glimpse a world where the extraordinary becomes ordinary, and the mundane transforms into the extraordinary. Through their stories, we are invited to consider the dynamic interplay between magic, craftsmanship, and the very essence of what it means to be human.

Chapter 10
Relationships and Interactions

The Tuatha Dé Danann and humans: Shared stories and connections
Bridging the Divine and Mortal Realms In the tapestry of Irish mythology, the interactions between the Tuatha Dé Danann, a race of supernatural beings, and humans create a rich and intricate narrative. These interactions not only reveal the complex relationships between different mythological entities but also highlight the blurred boundaries between the divine and mortal realms. This chapter delves into the shared stories and connections that exist between the Tuatha Dé Danann and humans, shedding light on the cultural significance of these interactions.

The Fomorian Rivalry and Human Alliances One of the key elements in the relationship between the Tuatha Dé Danann and humans is the presence of the Fomorians, another race of mythological beings. The Fomorians were often depicted as adversaries, engaging in battles with the Tuatha Dé Danann. In these clashes, humans occasionally played a role as allies or beneficiaries. For instance, the Tuatha Dé Danann sought the help of humans during their struggles against the Fomorians, establishing a connection that linked the fate of both races.

Balor of the Evil Eye The saga of Balor of the Evil Eye, a Fomorian king, exemplifies the intertwining of human and divine destinies. Balor's own lineage contained both Fomorian and Tuatha Dé Danann blood, reflecting the intricate nature of their relationships. Balor's grandson, Lugh Lámhfhada, emerged as a hero whose actions impacted both the divine and mortal realms.

Lugh's Rise to Heroism Lugh's dual heritage allowed him to bridge the gap between the two races. His presence within the Tuatha Dé Danann showcased a willingness to collaborate with humans, forging alliances and garnering respect from both sides. Lugh's involvement in the Battle of Magh Tuireadh, where he displayed exceptional skills, highlighted his pivotal role in shaping the shared history of the Tuatha Dé Danann and humans.

Marriage and Hybridity

The concept of marriage between members of the Tuatha Dé Danann and humans further emphasized the interconnectedness of these mythological races. Such unions often resulted in offspring who inherited qualities from both realms, showcasing a fusion of divine and mortal attributes. The tale of Aengus, a Tuatha Dé Danann god, and Caer Ibormeith, a human woman transformed into a swan, exemplifies the romantic connections that transcend the boundaries of the supernatural and human worlds. Aengus' determination to win Caer's heart demonstrated the depth of emotions that could be shared between beings from different realms.

Connla and the Forbidden Love The story of Connla, the son of the Tuatha Dé Danann god Lugh, and a woman from the mortal world reflects the challenges and obstacles faced by those who dared to cross the divide between the two realms. Connla's choice to follow his heart rather than societal expectations underscored the enduring themes of love and sacrifice.

The interactions between the Tuatha Dé Danann and humans in Irish mythology provide a tapestry of stories that resonate with universal themes of unity, love, and cooperation. These shared narratives remind us that the boundaries between the divine and mortal are not always rigid, and that connections forged between different worlds can yield both challenges and opportunities. The intertwining of destinies, the formation of alliances, and the portrayal of love across realms reveal the depth and complexity of human relationships, even in the realm of the fantastical. As we explore these stories, we come to appreciate the power of mythology to reflect and enrich our understanding of the human experience.

Chapter 11
Influence on Irish Culture

Traces of the Tuatha Dé Danann in literature and art

The Tuatha Dé Danann, the divine beings of Irish mythology, have left an indelible mark on Irish culture, permeating literature and art with their enchanting stories and timeless symbolism. As guardians of wisdom, magic, and craftsmanship, their influence extends far beyond ancient folklore, infusing modern Irish identity with layers of depth and mystique. The sagas and epics of Irish literature have become rich tapestries interwoven with the stories of the Tuatha Dé Danann. Their exploits in the Battle of Magh Tuireadh, where they clashed valiantly against the Fomorians, are recounted in epic poems and sagas like "Lebor Gabála Érenn" (The Book of Invasions). These narratives cast the Tuatha Dé Danann as heroes, embodying both the struggles and triumphs of Ireland's history. Perhaps the most iconic figure among them, Lugh Lámhfhada, takes center stage in tales of heroic quests and legendary feats. From his role as a master of many skills to his leadership on the battlefield, Lugh's character embodies the essence of Irish heroism and resourcefulness. These stories inspire a sense of cultural pride, underscoring the belief that the Tuatha Dé Danann's legacy continues to shape the Irish spirit.

Art: Mystical Renderings and Symbolic Imagery

The artistry of the Tuatha Dé Danann's influence is palpable in the visual expressions found in various forms of Irish art. Intricately adorned manuscripts, such as the Book of Kells, feature delicate illustrations depicting scenes of magic, transformation, and divine interaction. The symbols of their divine attributes, like the silver arm of Nuada or the harp of Dagda, are etched into the collective visual memory of the Irish people. There seems to be a connection between The Celtic harp and Dagda's Harp in Celtic mythology. Dagda's Harp is a legendary, magical harp associated with the Celtic god Dagda. This harp is often depicted as a harp of great beauty and power.

The connection between Dagda's Harp and the Celtic harp lies in their cultural and symbolic significance. The Celtic harp, also known as the clàrsach or Gaelic harp, is a traditional musical instrument that holds deep historical and cultural importance in Celtic regions, especially

Ireland and Scotland. Dagda's Harp is sometimes seen as a symbol of the Celtic harp, and it has influenced the way the harp is perceived and represented in Celtic culture. The harp, in general, has been a symbol of Irish and Scottish identity for centuries, appearing on flags, coins, and various emblems. It's often associated with music, storytelling, and cultural heritage. In this sense, Dagda's Harp serves as a mythological archetype that reflects the cultural reverence for the harp in Celtic traditions. While the two harps are distinct in terms of mythology and reality, they share a connection through their symbolic and cultural significance in Celtic history and heritage.

Beyond the pages of manuscripts, the Tuatha Dé Danann come to life in sculptures, paintings, and contemporary artworks. The delicate craftsmanship of metalwork and jewelry often features intricate designs inspired by their stories. The Sidhe, the Otherworldly realm of these divine beings, is rendered in ethereal landscapes that evoke a sense of wonder and reverence for the unseen. The presence of the Tuatha Dé Danann in literature and art bridges the gap between Ireland's ancient past and its modern identity. As cultural touchstones, they serve as a connection to a time when storytelling was both an entertainment and a vessel for passing down wisdom. This intergenerational transmission of stories reinforces a sense of cultural continuity, anchoring the Irish people to their roots. Moreover, the tales of the Tuatha Dé Danann speak to the deeply ingrained reverence for nature and the land. These themes resonate deeply in a country where the landscape is woven into the cultural fabric. The gods' relationship with the Otherworld, which parallels the spiritual connection between the living and the land, continues to shape perceptions of the world around us.

A Living Legacy
The Tuatha Dé Danann's influence on Irish culture endures as a testament to the enduring power of mythology. Through literature and art, they invite us to explore the realms of imagination, to celebrate heroism and resilience, and to ponder the mysteries of existence. Traces of their divine presence remind us that within the intricate tapestry of Irish culture, threads of myth and legend are intertwined, creating a vibrant and captivating narrative that continues to captivate and inspire.

Contemporary traditions inspired by Tuatha Dé Danann stories

Irish culture is deeply intertwined with mythology and folklore, with the stories of the Tuatha Dé Danann playing a significant role in shaping the collective identity of the Irish people. These ancient tales have transcended time, finding resonance in contemporary society through various traditions, celebrations, and cultural expressions. This article explores the enduring influence of Tuatha Dé Danann stories on modern Irish culture, examining how these narratives have woven themselves into the fabric of everyday life.

1. *Festivals and Celebrations:*

The tales of the Tuatha Dé Danann have left an indelible mark on Irish festivals and celebrations, with Imbolc being one of the most prominent examples. Imbolc, which marks the beginning of spring, is closely associated with the goddess Brigid. Her triple aspects as a goddess of fertility, poetry, and healing are celebrated during this festival. Many of the customs, such as lighting candles and making Brigid's crosses, directly harken back to the stories of the Tuatha Dé Danann. Imbolc not only connects modern-day Ireland to its mythological past but also fosters a sense of continuity and reverence for nature.

2. *Artistic Expression:*

The influence of Tuatha Dé Danann stories is palpable in Irish art, literature, and music. Numerous artists draw inspiration from these tales to create evocative visual representations, reflecting the magical and mystical aspects of the mythological beings. Furthermore, writers and poets often infuse their works with allusions to the Tuatha Dé Danann, contributing to the rich tapestry of Irish literary tradition. Musicians, too, are not exempt from this influence, with lyrical references to these ancient figures resonating in traditional and contemporary Irish music.

3. *Place Names and Landmarks:*

The influence of the Tuatha Dé Danann stories can even be traced in the geographical landscape of Ireland. Many place names and landmarks are directly linked to these ancient myths. Rivers, mountains, and valleys often carry names that evoke the mythological beings or events. These names not only enrich the landscape with a sense of enchantment but also serve as subtle reminders of the stories that have shaped the land's history and culture.

4. *Cultural Identity and Tourism:*
The enduring appeal of Tuatha Dé Danann stories contributes to the sense of cultural identity among the Irish people. These narratives, whether retold through festivals, art, or oral tradition, reinforce a unique cultural heritage that distinguishes Ireland on the global stage. Additionally, the allure of Irish mythology, including the Tuatha Dé Danann, attracts tourists and enthusiasts from around the world, promoting cultural exchange and appreciation.

The stories of the Tuatha Dé Danann continue to wield their enchanting influence over contemporary Irish culture. From festivals that honor Brigid's legacy to the threads of myth woven into art, literature, and local folklore, these ancient tales are more than stories of the past; they are living forces that shape and enrich the present. The enduring relevance of the Tuatha Dé Danann in modern Ireland highlights the power of mythology to bridge the gap between generations, foster a strong cultural identity, and remind society of the enduring magic that resides in the heart of Irish heritage.

The enduring impact on Irish identity and heritage
The beauty of Irish culture is intricately woven with the threads of mythology, legends, and ancient stories that have been passed down through generations. Among the most prominent and influential elements of Irish mythology are the Tuatha Dé Danann, a divine race of beings who have left an indelible mark on the cultural identity and heritage of Ireland. This essay delves into the enduring impact of the Tuatha Dé Danann on Irish culture, exploring how their stories, themes, and symbolism have shaped Irish identity and continue to resonate to this day. The Tuatha Dé Danann's influence extends beyond the national level, reaching into local and regional traditions across Ireland. Folktales, rituals, and customs rooted in the mythology of these divine beings can still be found in different corners of the country. These traditions serve as a reminder of the diverse ways in which the Tuatha Dé Danann have become interwoven with the daily lives of the Irish people.

Preservation of Cultural Heritage
The preservation of the Tuatha Dé Danann's stories and their integration into various aspects of Irish culture is a testament to the Irish people's commitment to safeguarding their cultural heritage. This preservation

underscores the importance of passing down ancestral knowledge and mythological narratives to future generations, reinforcing a sense of continuity and connection.

The Tuatha Dé Danann's enduring impact on Irish culture is a testament to the timeless power of myth to shape identity and inspire collective consciousness. Their stories serve as a repository of wisdom, values, and ideals that have influenced artistic expression, seasonal celebrations, and local traditions across Ireland. Through their influence, the Tuatha Dé Danann continue to weave their magic into the fabric of Irish identity, ensuring that the echoes of ancient myths resonate with every new dawn.

Chapter 12
Imbolc and Other Festivals

Imbolc: Origins and significance

Imbolc, celebrated on the 1st or 2nd of February, marks the beginning of spring and is a significant festival in Celtic mythology. Rooted in the ancient traditions of the Celtic peoples, Imbolc carries deep cultural and spiritual meanings, connecting communities to the rhythms of nature and the cycle of the seasons. In this essay, we will delve into the origins and significance of Imbolc, exploring how it reflects the Celtic worldview and its enduring impact on modern traditions. Imbolc finds its origins in the Gaelic word "Imbolg," meaning "in the belly," symbolizing the stirrings of life and growth beneath the Earth's surface as winter gives way to spring. The festival has its roots in the pre-Christian era, when Celtic societies were deeply intertwined with agricultural cycles and the natural world. Imbolc marks the halfway point between the winter solstice and the spring equinox, a time when the days gradually lengthen and the Earth awakens from its slumber.

Goddess Brigid: A Central Figure

Imbolc is closely associated with the Celtic goddess Brigid, who embodies aspects of fertility, creativity, and healing. Brigid, also known as Brigit or Bríd, is a triple goddess with various aspects representing different domains of life. She is the patroness of poets, artisans, and healers, symbolizing the interplay between inspiration, creation, and nurturing. Renewal and Rebirth: Imbolc celebrates the rebirth of nature after the cold, dark days of winter. The emergence of snowdrops and the lengthening daylight are seen as signs of renewal, offering hope and anticipation for the approaching spring. Imbolc is a time for purifying and cleansing one's surroundings. Rituals involving fire, water, and the burning of herbs are performed to cleanse not only physical spaces but also the spirit. This purification prepares individuals and communities for the new growth ahead. Imbolc is intimately connected to agriculture. It's a time when livestock would give birth to young, reflecting the life-giving force of nature. Ploughs were blessed to ensure a fruitful planting season, underscoring the importance of agricultural abundance.

Honoring Brigid

Imbolc is an occasion to honor the goddess Brigid. Temples and sacred fires were dedicated to her, and her role as a protector of hearth and home was acknowledged. Offerings of food and symbolic items were made to seek her blessings. Imbolc represents the liminal space between winter and spring, mirroring the broader Celtic concept of thresholds. It's a time when the potential for change and growth is embraced, making it an ideal period for personal reflection and setting intentions.

Modern Celebrations

While the traditional practices of Imbolc have evolved over time, the festival's spirit endures in modern celebrations. Some contemporary observances include:
- Lighting candles and fires to symbolize the return of light and warmth.
- Crafting "Brigid's crosses," woven from rushes, as protective symbols.
- Preparing meals featuring dairy products and early spring herbs.
- Engaging in creative pursuits and activities to honor Brigid's influence on the arts.

Imbolc, with its origins rooted in the ancient Celtic worldview, remains a cherished festival that celebrates the transition from winter to spring, the cycle of renewal, and the interconnectedness of humanity and nature. Its rituals and symbolism offer insights into the Celtic peoples' deep reverence for the natural world and their intimate relationship with the changing seasons. By embracing the lessons of Imbolc, modern celebrations continue to honor the spirit of growth, transformation, and the enduring legacy of Celtic traditions.

Brigid's role and associations with the festival

The changing seasons have long held profound significance in cultures across the world, giving rise to festivals that celebrate the cycles of nature and the interplay between the physical and the spiritual realms. Among these, the Celtic festival of Imbolc stands as a testament to the ancient reverence for the transition from winter to spring. At the heart of Imbolc lies the figure of Brigid, a goddess of multifaceted attributes who holds a special place in Celtic mythology and culture. Imbolc, often observed on February 1st or 2nd, marks the midpoint between the winter solstice and the vernal equinox. Derived from the Old Irish word "Imbolg," meaning "in the belly," the festival captures the anticipation of new life stirring beneath the surface of the earth, heralding the arrival of spring. This festival is deeply ingrained in Celtic tradition, symbolizing the rebirth of the land and the return of longer, sunlit days.

Brigid: The Triple Goddess

At the heart of Imbolc is the veneration of Brigid, a goddess known for her triadic nature. Brigid embodies three distinct yet interconnected aspects: Brigid the Healer, Brigid the Poet, and Brigid the Smith. Each facet reflects her role as a nurturer, a creator, and a protector. In Celtic tradition, Brigid seamlessly blends the spiritual with the practical, encapsulating the interconnectedness of life, art, and nature. Brigid's role in Imbolc is multifaceted, resonating with the themes of renewal and light that define the festival. As Brigid the Healer, she is invoked for blessings of health and well-being. This aspect of her persona emphasizes her connection to the life-giving forces of nature, as plants begin to sprout anew and the earth awakens from its slumber.

As Brigid the Poet, she is associated with inspiration, creativity, and the power of spoken word. In the spirit of Imbolc, when the world begins to reawaken, Brigid's influence is felt in the resurgence of artistic endeavors, poetic expressions, and the sharing of stories that celebrate the cycle of life and the changing seasons. Finally, Brigid the Smith underscores her connection to craftsmanship, particularly metalwork. This symbolism aligns with the festival's emphasis on the transition from the darkness of winter to the light of spring. Smithing, like the returning sunlight, is a transformative process that shapes raw materials into objects of beauty and utility. During Imbolc, various rituals and customs pay homage to Brigid's influence. Homes are cleansed and purified, symbolizing the shedding of old energies and the welcoming of new beginnings. Brigid's crosses, woven from straw or rushes, are hung in homes as protective talismans. These crosses embody Brigid's role as a guardian and defender, bridging the mundane and the divine. Offerings of food, milk, and even a bed are traditionally set out for Brigid to receive her blessings and ensure the prosperity of the household. The lighting of candles and fires during Imbolc symbolizes the return of the sun's warmth and the triumph of light over darkness.

Legacy and Modern Interpretations

Imbolc and its association with Brigid continue to captivate modern imaginations. The festival's celebration of renewal, creativity, and the transformative power of nature resonates with people seeking to reconnect with the rhythms of the earth. Many Neo-Pagan and Wiccan traditions incorporate Imbolc into their practices, often emphasizing Brigid's presence as a goddess of light and inspiration. Imbolc stands as a timeless testament to the cyclical nature of life and the importance of honoring transitions. At the heart of this festival, Brigid's role as the triple goddess reflects the interconnectedness of healing, artistry, and protection. Imbolc's rituals and customs celebrate the promise of spring, encouraging us to embrace new beginnings and the perennial cycle of growth that defines our world. Just as Brigid's multifaceted nature enriches Celtic mythology, her influence continues to inspire reverence and celebration in the modern world.

Other festivals and their connections to the Tuatha Dé Danann

Festivals play a pivotal role in connecting cultures to their ancient roots and celebrating the significant aspects of their mythologies. Spring Cleaning: Imbolc's association with purification led to a practice of spring-cleaning, both physical and spiritual, to prepare for the year ahead.

Beltane (May 1st): As the Tuatha Dé Danann embodied various aspects of nature, Beltane, marking the beginning of summer, is associated with their influence over the land's fertility. The Maypole dance echoes their connection to the Earth's vitality.

Lughnasadh (August 1st): Lughnasadh, a harvest festival, commemorates the god Lugh and his multifaceted talents. Celebrated with games, feasts, and gatherings, it acknowledges the harvest's bountiful results and reflects Lugh's attributes as a warrior, craftsman, and protector.

Samhain (October 31st - November 1st): As the veil between the mortal world and the Otherworld thins, Samhain provides a unique connection to the Tuatha Dé Danann. They, too, hailed from the Otherworld and are honored during this time of honoring ancestors and otherworldly beings.

Halloween

While Halloween, as it's celebrated today, has its origins in a mix of Celtic, Roman, and Christian traditions, there is some speculation that it may have distant connections to the ancient Celtic festival of Samhain. The Tuatha Dé Danann, as figures from Irish mythology, are associated with ancient Celtic culture, so there's an indirect link.

Samhain was a Celtic festival marking the end of the harvest season and the beginning of winter. It was believed that during this time, the boundaries between the living and the dead were blurred, allowing spirits to roam the earth. This idea of otherworldly beings and spirits returning may resonate with the Tuatha Dé Danann, who were considered supernatural beings. However, it's important to note that the direct connection between Halloween and the Tuatha Dé Danann is not a prominent part of Halloween's history or modern celebration. Halloween has evolved over the centuries and incorporated various influences, including Christian traditions like All Saints' Day (November 1st), and it has become a holiday focused on costumes, trick-or-treating, and other festivities. So, while there's a broader connection to Celtic and Irish folklore through Samhain, the Tuatha Dé Danann are not a central part of Halloween as it's commonly observed today.

Connections to the Tuatha Dé Danann

The thread of the Tuatha Dé Danann weaves through these festivals, connecting the divine with the mundane. These celebrations serve as an ongoing acknowledgment of the gods and goddesses, ensuring their influence remains alive in the hearts and minds of the people. The traditions, rituals, and symbolism associated with these festivals are a testament to the lasting impact of the Tuatha Dé Danann on the cultural identity of the Irish people. Imbolc and other seasonal festivals provide a tangible link to the Tuatha Dé Danann, infusing their mythology into the fabric of Celtic culture. These celebrations not only honor the divine attributes of the gods and goddesses but also foster a sense of continuity between the past and the present. By participating in these festivals, individuals and communities perpetuate the age-old stories of the Tuatha Dé Danann, celebrating their legacy and ensuring their influence remains vibrant and relevant in the modern world.

Chapter 13

Modern Interpretations

The Tuatha Dé Danann in modern literature and media

The legends of the Tuatha Dé Danann, the mythical beings from Irish folklore, have not only endured the test of time but have also found a captivating resonance in modern literature and media. The rich tapestry of their stories, with themes of heroism, magic, and a connection to the Otherworld, continues to captivate the imagination of creators and audiences alike. This chapter delves into the intricate web of modern interpretations surrounding the Tuatha Dé Danann, tracing their presence across literature, film, television, and other media forms. Modern interpretations of the Tuatha Dé Danann are a testament to their enduring relevance. These adaptations often draw from the ancient myths while giving them new life through contemporary lenses. Writers and creators have skillfully navigated the complexities of adapting ancient narratives to suit modern sensibilities, introducing these mythical beings to a new generation.

Literary Reimaginations

One of the most prominent areas of modern interpretation is literature. Authors such as Neil Gaiman, Morgan Llywelyn, and Marion Zimmer Bradley have woven the Tuatha Dé Danann into their works, adding layers of depth and complexity to these characters. Gaiman's "American Gods" introduces gods and mythological beings, including the Tuatha Dé Danann, into the fabric of contemporary America, exploring themes of belief, identity, and cultural clash.

Fantasy and Urban Fantasy

The genre of fantasy and urban fantasy has provided fertile ground for the integration of Tuatha Dé Danann into modern narratives. Their magical abilities, connections to the Otherworld, and rich backstories make them ideal inhabitants of fantastical worlds. Urban fantasy authors often reimagine these beings living alongside humans, navigating the challenges of modern life while retaining their mythological essence.

Film and Television

The visual medium of film and television has also embraced the allure of the Tuatha Dé Danann. The epic scope and dramatic potential of their stories have led to adaptations and interpretations on screen. The 2020 film "The Green Knight," directed by David Lowery, offers a fresh take on Arthurian legends, featuring the character of Gawain encountering the mystical and enigmatic Green Knight, often linked to the Tuatha Dé Danann.

Artistic and Artisanal Expression
Art and artisanal creations have provided a unique canvas for interpreting the Tuatha Dé Danann. Visual artists have reimagined these mythical beings through illustrations, paintings, and sculptures, capturing their otherworldly essence. Traditional crafts, such as jewelry and pottery, have incorporated symbols and motifs associated with the Tuatha Dé Danann, grounding their presence in tangible forms.

Gaming and Interactive Media
The realm of gaming and interactive media has offered a dynamic platform for engaging with the Tuatha Dé Danann. Video games, role-playing games, and online platforms have allowed players to immerse themselves in worlds where they interact with these mythological figures. This not only extends the reach of these stories but also encourages a deeper engagement with the lore and characters.

Modern interpretations of the Tuatha Dé Danann are a testament to the enduring power of mythology to shape and inspire creative expressions across various forms of media. Their presence in literature, film, art, and gaming not only pays homage to ancient legends but also fosters a continuous dialogue between the past and the present. As contemporary creators infuse new life into these mythical beings, the Tuatha Dé Danann stand as a reminder of the timeless allure of storytelling and the boundless possibilities of human imagination.

Reimaginings and adaptations in popular culture

The mythological tapestry of the Tuatha Dé Danann, deeply woven into the fabric of Irish culture, has not only endured through centuries but also evolved to find new life in the realm of modern popular culture. These ancient deities and their stories continue to captivate the imagination of artists, writers, filmmakers, and creators across various media. This segment delves into the intricate web of modern interpretations, reimaginings, and adaptations of the Tuatha Dé Danann, exploring how these mythological figures persistently influence and shape contemporary narratives. The mythology of the Tuatha Dé Danann, once transmitted orally and through ancient texts, has experienced a metamorphosis in the modern age. As societies evolved, the stories of these divine beings underwent transformations, acquiring new layers of interpretation, relevance, and cultural resonance. The timeless themes of heroism, sacrifice, and the interaction between humanity and the supernatural have provided fertile ground for creative exploration.

Literature: Breathing New Life into Old Tales

Contemporary literature has embraced the Tuatha Dé Danann as a wellspring of inspiration. Authors have skillfully reimagined these mythological beings in novel forms, melding ancient narratives with innovative storytelling techniques. Works like Marion Zimmer Bradley's "The Mists of Avalon" offer fresh perspectives on Arthurian legends through the lens of the Tuatha Dé Danann, infusing them with a renewed sense of magic and mystery. The themes of power struggles, alliances, and the Otherworldly resonate with readers seeking to explore the intersection of myth and reality.

Cinema: From Epic Battles to Character-Centric Dramas

The silver screen has not remained untouched by the allure of the Tuatha Dé Danann. Film adaptations have ranged from epic battles to intimate character-driven dramas, each exploring different facets of the mythology. "Song of the Sea" masterfully weaves Celtic folklore into a visually stunning animated narrative, introducing audiences to the enchanting world of selkies and other mystical creatures. By combining mythology with contemporary themes of family and identity, such adaptations manage to bridge the gap between ancient tales and modern sensibilities.

Television: Bringing Myth to the Masses

The episodic nature of television has provided creators with ample space to explore the intricacies of Tuatha Dé Danann myths. Series like "American Gods" incorporate these mythological figures into a larger narrative of gods existing in the modern world, reflecting on belief systems and the changing nature of worship. By juxtaposing ancient deities with contemporary society, such shows compel viewers to contemplate the relevance of myth in their lives and cultural contexts.

Visual Arts: Rediscovering Aesthetic Splendor

Visual artists have reinvigorated the Tuatha Dé Danann through stunning depictions that capture both their divine essence and their intricate relationships. Paintings, sculptures, and digital art reinterpret key moments in mythology, allowing audiences to engage with the mythos on a sensory level. These creations often merge the ethereal qualities of the Tuatha Dé Danann with modern artistic techniques, culminating in a visual feast that transports viewers to realms both ancient and new.

Music and Performance: Enchanting Audiences

Music and performance arts offer unique avenues for modern interpretations of the Tuatha Dé Danann. Musicians draw from mythological themes to craft enchanting melodies and lyrical journeys that evoke the magic of the Otherworld. Additionally, theater and dance performances infused with elements of Tuatha Dé Danann myths provide audiences with immersive experiences, blurring the boundaries between reality and the supernatural.

A Continual Resurgence

The Tuatha Dé Danann, a treasure trove of mythical figures and stories, continues to inspire and ignite the creativity of modern creators across various mediums. From literature and cinema to visual arts and music, their presence remains ever-present in the cultural landscape. These contemporary adaptations not only pay homage to ancient traditions but also breathe new life into these narratives, ensuring that the legacy of the Tuatha Dé Danann lives on, resonating with each generation and reaffirming the enduring power of myth.

Continuing relevance and fascination with ancient myths

Ancient myths hold an enduring fascination that transcends time and culture. Among these myths, the tales of the Tuatha Dé Danann, the supernatural beings of Irish mythology, continue to captivate modern audiences. The modern interpretations of these ancient stories reveal the remarkable staying power of these narratives and shed light on the ways in which they resonate with contemporary sensibilities. The preservation of ancient myths, including those of the Tuatha Dé Danann, has been facilitated by literature, folklore, and cultural practices. From the medieval manuscripts to oral traditions, these myths have been passed down through generations, maintaining their allure and mystique. In recent decades, there has been a resurgence of interest in traditional folklore and mythology, with efforts to revitalize these tales through books, films, and even festivals. This revival speaks to the timeless appeal of the Tuatha Dé Danann stories and their ability to evoke a sense of connection with ancestral heritage.

Archetypes and Universality

One reason for the ongoing relevance of these myths is their exploration of universal themes and archetypes. The Tuatha Dé Danann narratives touch on themes such as heroism, sacrifice, power struggles, and the interplay between mortals and the divine. These themes are not bound by time or culture; they resonate with human experiences and emotions across eras. As individuals grapple with personal challenges and societal changes, the struggles and triumphs of gods and heroes offer a mirror through which to reflect on their own lives. Modern literature and media have provided a platform for reimagining and adapting ancient myths, infusing them with contemporary perspectives. Authors, filmmakers, and artists have drawn inspiration from the Tuatha Dé Danann stories, crafting narratives that explore the nuances of character relationships, motivations, and psychological depths. These adaptations often blend the mysticism of the past with the sensibilities of the present, resulting in a fresh and relatable interpretation of the myths.

Cultural Identity and Connection

The Tuatha Dé Danann myths hold a special place in the hearts of those with Irish heritage. They serve as a link to the past, a reminder of the rich cultural legacy that has shaped their identity. As the world becomes increasingly interconnected, individuals seek anchors to their roots, and ancient myths provide a means of connecting with the ancestral and cultural heritage. The retelling of these myths reinforces a sense of belonging and reminds individuals of the values and traditions that continue to influence their lives.

Inspiration for Creativity
The Tuatha Dé Danann myths have become a wellspring of inspiration for artists across various mediums. From visual arts to music, creators draw from the symbolism, imagery, and narratives to produce works that evoke emotions and stimulate the imagination. The magical realms, heroic quests, and intricate relationships woven into these myths provide fertile ground for creative exploration, enabling artists to breathe new life into age-old stories.

The continuing relevance and fascination with the ancient myths of the Tuatha Dé Danann underscore the timeless nature of these narratives. Their ability to transcend temporal and cultural boundaries speaks to the fundamental human desire to explore the mysteries of existence, grapple with complex emotions, and find meaning in the ever-changing world. As modern interpretations intertwine with ancient lore, the stories of the Tuatha Dé Danann persist as a testament to the enduring power of mythology in shaping our understanding of ourselves and the world around us.

Chapter 14

Unanswered Questions and Speculations

Gaps in the mythology: Exploring mysteries and uncertainties
Irish mythology is a realm of wonder, magic, and intrigue, filled with gods, goddesses, and epic tales that have captured the imagination of generations. Among the prominent figures in this mythology are the Tuatha Dé Danann, a divine race known for their advanced skills, otherworldly origins, and significant impact on Irish culture. While their stories are rich and captivating, they are not without their enigmas and unanswered questions, leaving room for speculation and exploration.

1. *Mysterious Origins:* One of the central mysteries surrounding the Tuatha Dé Danann lies in their origins. While it is established that they descended from the heavens to Ireland, the details of this arrival remain unclear. Were they extraterrestrial beings, symbols of a celestial connection, or perhaps representations of an ancient people's mythic interpretation of historical events? Speculation abounds regarding the nature of their arrival and what it might signify.

2. *The Vanishing of Nuada:* The fate of Nuada after the Battle of Magh Tuireadh raises questions that invite contemplation. Nuada's silver arm, a symbol of resilience and kingship, was severed in battle, leading to his demise. Yet, there are no accounts of his journey to the afterlife or his continued presence in the Otherworld. Speculation could explore the possibility of Nuada's continued influence beyond his earthly life, perhaps as a guiding force for his people.

3. *Intermingling with Mortals:* The interactions between the Tuatha Dé Danann and humans offer fertile ground for speculation. How did these divine beings and mortals cross paths, and what implications did these encounters have on human history? Were they benevolent teachers or enigmatic figures influencing the course of events? The blurred lines between the realms of gods and humans invite imaginative exploration into the reasons behind these interactions.

4. *The Enigma of the Sidhe:* The Tuatha Dé Danann are often associated with the Otherworld, particularly the mystical realm of the Sidhe. Yet, the nature of the Sidhe and its relationship to the mortal realm remain shrouded in mystery. Speculation could delve into the symbolism of the

Sidhe, exploring its connections to death, rebirth, and the cyclical nature of existence, as well as its representation as a bridge between realms.

5. *The Fate of Lost Deities:* While the major figures of the Tuatha Dé Danann pantheon are well-known, there are hints of lesser-known deities whose stories have been lost to time. Speculation could center on these forgotten or overshadowed gods and goddesses, contemplating their potential roles and significance, and offering creative interpretations of their stories.

6. *Cross-Cultural Connections:* The Tuatha Dé Danann share some characteristics with mythological beings from other cultures. Speculation could explore potential cross-cultural connections, reflecting on shared archetypes, myths, and themes that resonate across different mythologies. Were the Tuatha Dé Danann unique to Celtic culture, or do they share common roots with other ancient pantheons?

7. *Modern-Day Resonance:* Speculation could extend to the modern era, considering the enduring appeal of the Tuatha Dé Danann and their stories. How have these ancient myths evolved to remain relevant in contemporary times? What can their tales teach us about human nature, resilience, and the interplay between the mortal and divine?

The Tuatha Dé Danann, while captivating in their mythological narratives, offer a canvas for speculation and exploration. Unanswered questions and gaps in the mythology provide an opportunity for imaginative inquiry into their origins, interactions, and significance. As we unravel the mysteries surrounding these divine beings, we find that the gaps in the mythology are not voids to be filled, but gateways to deeper understanding, creativity, and connection to the essence of Irish culture and the universal human experience.

The myths and legends surrounding the Tuatha Dé Danann, the enigmatic group of supernatural beings from Irish mythology, have captured the imagination of scholars and enthusiasts for centuries. While these tales provide glimpses into their extraordinary abilities and interactions, a veil of mystery still shrouds their origins and ultimate purpose. This chapter delves into the realm of unanswered questions and speculative theories that attempt to shed light on the elusive aspects of the Tuatha Dé Danann.

1. *Origins in Pre-Celtic Beliefs:* One compelling theory posits that the Tuatha Dé Danann might be remnants of pre-Celtic deities and beings, assimilated into Celtic mythology over time. This perspective suggests that their origin lies in ancient animistic beliefs of the land and its spirits, which later became integrated into Celtic culture.

2. *An Atlantean Connection:* Some theorists propose a link between the Tuatha Dé Danann and the lost civilization of Atlantis. This speculative connection draws parallels between advanced civilizations and magical prowess, suggesting that the Tuatha Dé Danann could be survivors or descendants of Atlantis, bringing their advanced knowledge to Ireland.

3. *Cosmic Ancestry:* Another intriguing speculation delves into cosmic ancestry, suggesting that the Tuatha Dé Danann could be celestial beings who descended to Earth from distant star systems or higher dimensions. This theory attempts to explain their supernatural abilities and mysterious origins through an extraterrestrial lens.

4. *Interactions with Ancient Humans:* Several myths hint at interactions between the Tuatha Dé Danann and humans. Speculation arises that they might have played a role in human history, aiding or guiding early human civilizations. This theory connects their purpose to nurturing human development and guiding them toward progress.

5. *Guardians of the Land:* The Tuatha Dé Danann are often associated with the land and nature. Some theorists propose that they might represent guardian spirits of the Irish landscape, embodying the energies and forces of the natural world. Their purpose could be to maintain the balance between nature and humanity.
6. *Spiritual Archetypes:* Speculation also surrounds the idea that the Tuatha Dé Danann could embody archetypal representations of human

qualities and forces of nature. Each god or goddess might symbolize a specific aspect of human experience, such as wisdom, bravery, or creativity. In this view, their purpose is to teach and inspire through symbolic stories.

7. *Lessons and Moral Teachings:* The stories of the Tuatha Dé Danann often contain moral lessons and ethical dilemmas. Some theorists suggest that their purpose might be to serve as allegorical figures, imparting wisdom and moral guidance to humanity through their myths and actions.

The Tuatha Dé Danann remain a subject of fascination and speculation, as their origins and purpose continue to elude definitive explanation. While each theory presents a unique perspective, the mystery surrounding these divine beings adds to the richness of Irish mythology. Whether rooted in pre-Celtic beliefs, cosmic connections, or spiritual archetypes, the speculative theories remind us of the enduring power of mythology to inspire imagination and exploration. As we continue to unravel the enigma of the Tuatha Dé Danann, we uncover not only their hidden origins but also the depths of human curiosity and storytelling ingenuity.

Conclusion

Key takeaways from the journey into Tuatha Dé Danann mythology
As we conclude our immersive journey into the realm of Tuatha Dé Danann mythology, it becomes evident that their tales hold a tapestry woven with threads of heroism, magic, sacrifice, and enduring cultural significance. Through the layers of enchanting narratives and ancient symbolism, several key takeaways emerge, offering insights into the profound impact of these mythological figures on both the ancient Celtic world and the modern imagination. The Tuatha Dé Danann stand as guardians of Ireland's rich cultural identity and heritage. Their stories, spanning generations, have been integral to the formation of a collective Irish consciousness. Across millennia, these narratives have been shared around hearths and celebrated in festivals, serving as a testament to the enduring connection between mythology and cultural preservation. The Tuatha Dé Danann's presence in literature, art, and contemporary traditions demonstrates how ancient tales continue to shape and define a nation's character.

The gods and goddesses of the Tuatha Dé Danann embody timeless human qualities, making them relatable archetypes that transcend epochs. The journey of Nuada, with his silver arm symbolizing resilience after loss, reflects the universal human struggle to overcome adversity. Lugh's multifaceted skills encompass qualities sought after by individuals and societies alike: bravery, intelligence, and creativity. Brigid's triadic nature captures the complexities of feminine power, nurturing, and inspiration. These archetypes allow individuals to find elements of themselves within the mythic narratives, forging a personal connection to the ancient past. One of the most profound takeaways is the intricate interplay between the mortal realm and the Otherworld. The Tuatha Dé Danann's residence in the Sidhe and their interactions with humans underscore the belief in a symbiotic relationship between realms. This interconnectedness highlights the ancient Celtic worldview, where the veil between worlds is thin, and supernatural forces influence the everyday lives of mortals. Exploring this concept, we realize that the mythological tales provide a framework for understanding the mystical dimensions of existence that extend beyond the mundane.

Enduring Themes and Lessons
Delving into the myths, we discover timeless themes and lessons that continue to resonate. The Battle of Magh Tuireadh's depiction of

courage, sacrifice, and collaboration showcases the eternal struggle between good and evil, highlighting the importance of unity in the face of adversity. Nuada's acceptance of a silver arm emphasizes the transformative power of adaptation and acceptance in the wake of challenges. The themes of stewardship, craftsmanship, and wisdom embedded in these stories remind us of the reverence ancient societies held for nature and knowledge. The Tuatha Dé Danann myths offer a treasure trove of interpretations and insights, perpetually enriching our understanding. Their enigmatic nature, coupled with gaps in the narratives, invites continual exploration and speculation. The legends' flexibility allows us to engage with them from various angles, fostering a dynamic relationship between past and present. Scholars, artists, and enthusiasts alike continue to reinterpret these tales, reinvigorating their relevance for each generation.

Our journey into Tuatha Dé Danann mythology is not a conclusion but an invitation to curiosity and ongoing discovery. These tales are not static relics of the past; rather, they are living narratives that breathe life into cultural dialogues, artistic endeavors, and spiritual quests. By engaging with the Tuatha Dé Danann's stories, we embrace a lifelong odyssey of unraveling layers of meaning and connection.
Our exploration of Tuatha Dé Danann mythology has unraveled a rich tapestry of cultural heritage, human experience, and metaphysical wonder. Their tales, spanning time and space, transcend boundaries to remind us that myths are not mere stories but mirrors reflecting the intricate tapestries of human existence. The journey into their world leaves us with the profound realization that within myth lies an eternal wellspring of wisdom, inspiration, and the eternal quest to understand the boundless mysteries of our existence.

Theories about the Tuatha Dé Danann's origins and purpose
As we come to the culmination of this exploration into the captivating realm of the Tuatha Dé Danann, we find ourselves standing at the crossroads of ancient mythology and modern imagination. The journey through the rich tapestry of their tales has illuminated the profound allure and timeless significance that these stories continue to hold. In this concluding reflection, we will delve into the reasons behind the enduring allure of the Tuatha Dé Danann's narratives and their profound impact on the fabric of cultural heritage. The stories of the Tuatha Dé Danann function as the cornerstone of Irish cultural heritage. As these myths

have been passed down through generations, they have played a pivotal role in preserving and shaping the identity of the Irish people. The divine pantheon of gods and goddesses represents not only a supernatural world but also a mirror to the human experience. The challenges, sacrifices, and triumphs of the Tuatha Dé Danann resonate on a deeply human level, reminding us of the complexities and potentials of our own lives.

Embedded within the narratives of the Tuatha Dé Danann are universal themes that transcend time and culture. The pursuit of wisdom, the struggles for justice, the resilience in the face of adversity, and the power of unity are themes that resonate with humanity throughout history. The symbolism of Nuada's silver arm, Lugh's multifaceted abilities, and Brigid's nurturing presence encapsulates archetypal aspects of the human journey, inviting us to contemplate our own roles in the grand tapestry of existence. The allure of the Tuatha Dé Danann's stories lies in their ability to inspire boundless imagination. These tales have acted as a wellspring of creativity for countless artists, writers, and thinkers over the centuries. From poetry to visual art, from literature to music, the stories of the Tuatha Dé Danann have offered a fertile ground for the exploration of the mystical and the magical. Their narratives spark curiosity, inviting us to ponder the mysteries of the cosmos, the connection between mortals and the divine, and the enigmatic realm of the Otherworld.

Relevance in Modern Times
In a world characterized by rapid change and technological advancement, the stories of the Tuatha Dé Danann offer an anchor to a past where the sacred and the mundane were intertwined. The lessons derived from their trials and tribulations remain poignant in contemporary times. Their stories remind us that leadership requires sacrifice, that knowledge and craftsmanship hold transformative power, and that the pursuit of harmony with the environment is a noble endeavor. As we conclude this journey through the myths and legends of the Tuatha Dé Danann, we do not bid farewell, but rather extend an invitation for further exploration. The allure of these stories lies not only in their retelling but also in their reinterpretation. Just as the poets of old wove new verses around ancient themes, we, too, are called upon to engage with the legacy of the Tuatha Dé Danann, to seek deeper meanings, and to share their tales with generations to come.

In the intricate threads of these stories, we find an exquisite mosaic of human nature, aspirations, and the profound connections that bind us across time and space. The enduring allure of the Tuatha Dé Danann's narratives serves as a testament to the enduring power of storytelling and its ability to bridge the gap between past, present, and future. May we continue to draw inspiration from these myths, finding in their ageless magic a wellspring of wisdom and wonder for generations yet to come.

Invitation to continue exploring and interpreting Irish mythology
Throughout the pages of this book, we have embarked on a captivating journey into the enchanting realm of Irish mythology, with a particular focus on the enigmatic figures of the Tuatha Dé Danann. As we draw this narrative to a close, it is not an end, but rather a beckoning to further exploration and interpretation of the rich tapestry of Irish myths that continue to captivate hearts and minds across generations. The Tuatha Dé Danann, with their complex stories, symbolisms, and profound impact on culture, serve as a gateway to the wider realm of Irish mythology—a realm that invites us to delve deeper and to discover the enduring truths that lie beneath the surface. The tales of the Tuatha Dé Danann are not mere relics of the past; they are living entities that have transcended time. Irish mythology, with its vivid characters and vivid landscapes, has the power to resonate with our modern sensibilities, offering profound insights into the human condition, the mysteries of existence, and the dynamic interplay between mortals and the divine. These myths, like whispers from the past, remind us that the questions, hopes, and fears of ancient times are not so dissimilar from our own. One of the most remarkable aspects of mythology is its ability to accommodate a multitude of interpretations. As we look upon the tales of the Tuatha Dé Danann, we encounter layers upon layers of meaning that can be unpacked, each unveiling new insights. The silver arm of Nuada, for instance, speaks not only of resilience in the face of adversity, but also of the sacrifices leaders make for the greater good. Similarly, Lugh's multifaceted attributes reveal the heroism within us all, waiting to be harnessed for the betterment of our world.

Exploring the Shadows and the Light
The beauty of mythology lies in its willingness to explore both the shadows and the light within the human psyche. The Tuatha Dé Danann embody

this duality, showcasing heroic deeds alongside moments of vulnerability and imperfection. These contrasts mirror the complexity of our own lives, reminding us that we, too, possess the capacity for greatness and fallibility. By engaging with these stories, we not only find solace in shared struggles, but also inspiration in shared triumphs.
The conclusion of this book does not signal the end of our exploration but, rather, a transition to a new chapter in our ongoing relationship with Irish mythology. The Tuatha Dé Danann invite us to delve into their stories anew, to reimagine their tales in ways that resonate with our own experiences, and to extract lessons that can guide us in navigating the challenges of our times. Just as the heroes and heroines of old confronted adversity with courage, we, too, can draw strength from their narratives as we navigate our modern world.

Shaping the Future As we step forward, let us remember that mythology is not static; it is a dynamic force that evolves as we engage with it. By interpreting and reimagining these stories, we honor the cultural heritage of Ireland while also shaping its future. Just as the bards of old wove new variations of myths to suit their audiences, we have the opportunity to contribute to the ongoing narrative of Irish mythology, adding our voices to the chorus that spans centuries.

In the grand tapestry of Irish mythology, the stories of the Tuatha Dé Danann are but a single thread, interconnected with countless others. As we conclude our exploration, let us heed the call to continue weaving the fabric of this enduring tradition. By embracing the legacy of the Tuatha Dé Danann and embracing the spirit of exploration, interpretation, and reimagination, we become part of a timeless tradition—a tradition that reminds us of our shared humanity, our collective imagination, and our boundless capacity for wonder.

A Legacy of Inspiration and Wonder
The tales of the Tuatha Dé Danann are not just stories of gods and heroes; they are invitations to awaken our sense of wonder, curiosity, and

imagination. As we journey through life, we are reminded that there are mysteries yet to be unraveled, realms yet to be explored, and insights yet to be discovered. Just as the Tuatha Dé Danann navigated the realms of the mortal and the Otherworldly, we, too, can venture into the realms of knowledge and creativity. One of the enduring qualities of mythology is its ability to foster dialogue and encourage diverse perspectives. The Tuatha Dé Danann's stories invite us to see the world through different lenses, to consider the interplay of light and shadow, and to question the boundaries between reality and imagination. As we engage with these narratives, we join a lineage of thinkers, artists, and dreamers who have contributed to the rich tapestry of human thought. Irish mythology thrives not only in academia but also in art, literature, music, and other creative forms. It inspires poets to pen verses that capture the essence of heroes, ignites the brushstrokes of painters who depict magical landscapes, and weaves melodies that echo the songs of ancient bards. By participating in this creative dialogue, we contribute to a living legacy that resonates with audiences across the world and across time.

A Bridge Between Generations
In our journey through the stories of the Tuatha Dé Danann, we bridge the gap between past and present, forging connections between generations. These narratives, passed down through the ages, remind us that we are part of a greater continuum—a story that began long before us and will continue long after. By exploring the tales of the Tuatha Dé Danann, we honor the wisdom of those who came before and lay the foundation for those who will follow. As we embrace the invitation to explore and interpret Irish mythology, we embark on a journey of personal growth and self-discovery. The myths, like mirrors, reflect aspects of ourselves that we may not yet recognize. They challenge us to confront our fears, cultivate our strengths, and navigate the complexities of our own lives with resilience and purpose.

A New Beginning
As we conclude this book and bid farewell to the enchanting world of the Tuatha Dé Danann, we are reminded that every ending marks the

beginning of a new chapter. The journey of exploring Irish mythology and the tales of these divine beings is not finite; it is a cycle that continues to renew itself with each generation that discovers their stories anew. The Tuatha Dé Danann extend an open invitation to us all: an invitation to unearth hidden treasures, to seek out wisdom, and to find echoes of our own stories in the myths of old. The conclusion reflects on the lasting wonder and significance of the Tuatha Dé Danann's stories, drawing upon their preservation of identity, universal themes, inspiration, relevance, and the invitation for further exploration. It underscores the timelessness of mythology and its ability to resonate with humanity across ages and cultures.

So, dear reader, as you close this book and step back into the modern world, know that the magic and wonder of the Tuatha Dé Danann travel with you. The call to explore, interpret, and reimagine their stories remains alive—a call to become part of a timeless tradition, to honor the past, and to shape the future. The realm of Irish mythology awaits your exploration, your interpretation, and your creative contribution. Embrace the journey, for it is an invitation to connect with the eternal heart of human experience and the enduring power of imagination.

Printed in Great Britain
by Amazon